Elizabeth Godfrey

Cornish Diamonds

Elizabeth Godfrey

Cornish Diamonds

ISBN/EAN: 9783743323131

Manufactured in Europe, USA, Canada, Australia, Japa

Cover: Foto ©ninafisch / pixelio.de

Manufactured and distributed by brebook publishing software (www.brebook.com)

Elizabeth Godfrey

Cornish Diamonds

BY
Elizabeth Godfrey,
Author of
"*'Twixt Wood and Sea.*"

In Two Volumes.
Vol. II.

LONDON:
RICHARD BENTLEY & SON,
PUBLISHERS IN ORDINARY
TO HER MAJESTY THE QUEEN.
1895.
(All rights reserved.)

BOOK II.

(Continued.)

CORNISH DIAMONDS.

CHAPTER V.

THE summer weeks went by, hastened in their passage by an amount of amusement rare at Kerranstow. The weather was unusually settled and steady for the west coast, and most of the inhabitants had friends staying with them. After his old college friend, Mr. Jaques had the Wynnstays for a few weeks, and one of Mrs. Dendron's pretty sisters alighted for a flying visit at Pencoct; so of course all these people must be amused and have all the beauties of the neighbourhood displayed to them. A golf-ground was started on the stretch of moorland beyond Hennacombe, and hardly a week passed that the whole of the little society did not unite in a day's excursion to some distant spot, supposed to possess greater attractions of some kind than their own splendid bit of coast. Even busy Rachel laid aside a few of her tasks, at the risk of letting her parochial machinery get out of gear, and gave herself up to the idle enjoyment that was the order of the day.

Alick Studland was recovering, and no longer looked the gaunt scarecrow that he had been on his first arrival, but he was by no means yet in condition for service, and was enjoying to the full the *dolce far niente* of convalescence. His intimacy at Pencoet had gone on growing without let or hindrance, and it was a long time before it excited any remark. It seemed natural enough that he, having such abundant leisure, should visit constantly at the pleasantest house in the neighbourhood, and that he should pay to its mistress all those little attentions that seemed her due—that he should sit at her feet at the *al fresco* lunches, should stroll about with her, fetch and carry for her, and be ready to attend on all her caprices. Her supremacy in whatever company she happened to be was always so incontestable that for a long time no one thought of making any comment. Kerranstow was slow to think evil; but there arrived a time, when August was ripening into September, when people began to watch them, to look at each other and exchange remarks, when, in short, it began to be remembered that there was such a person as Oliver Dendron in existence, and this was beginning to look like a matter of which he might be expected to take cognizance.

It was difficult to say how the idea first took shape; probably in the brain of Mrs. Twisselton; but once started, it could not be ignored. Possibly her senses were sharpened by finding herself always at some disadvantage in the little society of Kerranstow. In spite of the desire of everybody to be as civil as possible to her, she was conscious that, in some way she could not define, she was not one of them. She was a woman who liked to be first, and here she found herself always a bad third, and it annoyed her. It also left her more at leisure for making her own observations.

It was at a picnic to Gooseburn Mills that she first set the ball rolling. It was the scene of the shipwreck of two winters ago, and here there was a beach and a little sandy cove that made boating possible, and it was always a delight to the upland folk to be able to enjoy the sea at close quarters. Letty was alone now, her sister having started for Homburg the week before, and, not caring to have the carriage out for her sole use, she had declared her intention of riding. Naturally enough, Alick proposed himself as her escort, and, as they would be part of quite a cavalcade of dogcarts, etc., no objection could be made by Mrs. Grundy. They thought good, however, to take a short cut over the turf, which, like most short cuts, resulted in their not arriving till every one was seated round the tablecloth, discussing cold pie and mayonnaise.

Nothing was said at the time, beyond a little

good-humoured chaffing of Alick for not knowing the way better, and it was not till after lunch, when the party had broken up into twos and threes, that Mrs. Twisselton had an opportunity of relieving her conscience. She did not choose her confidante very judiciously. She and Rachel had strolled down to the edge of the receding tide, and, poking the fringe of wet brown seaweed with the point of her parasol, she remarked—

"Well, I must say I do wonder at Mr. Dendron, don't you?"

"Why?" said Rachel, absently, wondering whether those two figures at the other horn of the bay, pushing down a boat, were Alick and Letty, and whether Jenifer or the Wynnstays were going too.

"Why!" repeated Mrs. Twisselton, with a laugh. "The idea of his letting his wife go flacketing about by herself in this fashion. Well, if anything happens, he has only himself to thank."

Rachel was furious, and none the less because in her secret soul it had occurred to her to wonder whether her brother might not be going a little too far—presuming too much on the immunities and unconventionalities of country life—and whether she could venture to warn him. Besides her natural indignation at having the idea thus coarsely presented, she was wroth at Mrs. Twisselton having the effrontery to speak to her on a matter in which a member of her own family was involved.

"I imagine Mr. and Mrs. Dendron understand each other perfectly well," she said coldly. "He does not care at all for these sort of excursions. If by 'anything happening' you mean that she might have lost her way this morning, you forget she was with my brother."

But it was useless to think Mrs. Twisselton could feel any snubs through her tough hide, and, with another little sarcastic laugh, she said—

"Oh, you don't understand what I mean. If she does not take care, she may lose her way with Mr. Studland in more senses than one."

Rachel made no answer, and began to walk away, but before she had gone many steps she encountered the vicar, who approached them, saying—

"Miss Treby, are you and Mrs. Twisselton inclined for a row over to Seal Island? We shall just have time before tea, if we start promptly. By the way, have you any idea what has become of the others—Studland and Mrs. Dendron, I mean? The rest are down by the boat. I thought, if we all went, we had better take two boats. What do you say?"

But Mrs. Twisselton, with a glance of exultant malice at Rachel, responded promptly—

"Oh, we saw Mrs. Dendron and her cavalier push off in a little skiff just now; didn't we, Miss Treby?"

"Ah, well," said Mr. Jaques, placidly, "I dare say we shall find them over on the island."

But the truants were not on Seal Island; neither were they discoverable when the rest returned to the cove at five o'clock. The kettle was boiled, the tea-things were unpacked, and still there was not a sign of them.

"Never mind. Tea is sure to bring them," said Muriel, merrily, helping Jenifer to set out cups and saucers. "Mrs. Dendron won't miss her afternoon tea if she can help it."

Rachel was uneasy, though she tried not to show it. She was anxious lest Alick should have overtaxed his strength, and be unable to row back against the strong tide now running out, and she was doubly uncomfortable as she recalled Mrs. Twisselton's unpleasant innuendoes. There was no one with whom she could take counsel but Jenifer, and to her she could say nothing till tea was over and together they carried a pile of crockery down to a brook, out of hearing of the others, to wash up.

"It is very odd," she began, "that Letty and Alick should not have got back yet; don't you think so? I hope they have not got into any difficulties with that boat."

"Oh, I don't think anything could have happened to them in this weather, and Mr. Studland understands what he is about too well to do anything foolish. It is not like you to be nervous."

Rachel smiled. "No, I am not given to tremors;

but the fact is, I am a little uneasy. It is not so much that I am afraid of their having come to grief; but I wonder whether you have noticed—you are so much more at Pencoet than I am—has it ever struck you that—well, in short, that Alick is there too much?"

Jenifer finished very carefully wiping the cup that Rachel handed her, before she answered in a steady, level voice—

"I haven't been there myself so often lately. I suppose it is natural he should go there a good deal. He isn't strong enough for golf yet or a long day's shooting, and there isn't much else for him to do."

"That is true; but still that does not justify them in going off like this together away from all the rest of us. I don't like it, Jenifer; it makes me uncomfortable."

Neither did Jenifer, and still less did she like being called upon to discuss the matter; but there was a good deal of resolute stuff in her, and she faced the situation unflinchingly.

"They are great friends, certainly; nobody could help noticing that; but one need not suppose there is any harm in it."

"Harm in it!" said Rachel, irritably. "You have seen nothing of the world, Jenifer, and it is all very well for you to take that innocent view; but they are both quite old enough, and worldly enough, to know what people would be likely to say; and you can see for yourself that if any unmarried girl carried on in that style we should all suppose they were engaged."

Jenifer found herself, she knew not why, embarked on the cause of the defence. She could not but admit the force of Rachel's last argument; but added—

"You know I think Letty would always know how to take care of herself, and not go too far."

"H'm. I doubt whether Alick is equally well-armed. But I must say I think it is entirely her doing."

Jenifer thought so too, but that was a topic on which she would rather keep silence. She finished piling up the cups, and rose to carry them back; but before they rejoined the others, Rachel said—

"The worst of it is people are beginning to notice and comment. If your cousin says anything to you about it, snap her up, won't you?"

Jenifer nodded acquiescence, and the subject was dropped. As they went up the beach, a little boat containing two people came in sight, slowly rounding the headland to the northward.

The two delinquents had drifted away together between the sea and the sunshine, heedless of the proprieties, careless of the company they left behind, only desiring to enjoy the blue unclouded weather in their own fashion and in each others' society, which for the moment they preferred to any other.

"Shall we go to Seal Island?" asked Studland, as he pushed off. "We may perhaps catch a glimpse of a seal taking his afternoon siesta on the sunny side."

"No, that is too commonplace; everybody goes to Seal Island. Let us go after those birds."

She pointed to a spot to the northward, where a school of mackerel had drawn together a crowd of sea-birds from every point in the compass. Gulls, cormorants, guillemots were all circling, swooping, flapping over the space of troubled water with hoarse, shrill cries.

"How delicious it is to get away!" said Letty, trailing her bare hand childishly through the water. "How I hate a picnic, don't you?"

"Why?" He had reached that point of intimacy when he felt he might talk in monosyllables if he chose.

"It is so ridiculous when you have discovered a perfectly wild and lovely spot, where solitude is the essence of the charm, and have taken the trouble to transport yourself there with provisions for the whole day, to spoil it all by collecting together all the most boring elements of society."

"But I thought you liked society. I have heard you pity yourself for being out of the world."

"Stupid boy. I should have thought you understood me better. This"—pointing to the group still visible in the bay behind her—"is not the world; still less is it Society—with a big S, mark—I like things in extremes; I like the cream of society, crowded functions, gorgeous festivities; or, failing that, I like solitude—*solitude à deux.*"

"I am glad you put in that saving clause. I should not like to think you did not want me; or wanted me only as a pair of arms."

"Ah," said she, "one mayn't be always in the mood for one's acquaintances, but one always wants one's friends."

"Thank you."

Their eyes met, and Letty felt it would be wiser not to pursue that subject any farther just then.

She was just beginning to be aware that the ice was getting rather thin, and was trying not to see a board in front of her, marked "dangerous." The guise of simplicity and friendliness which her flirtations always wore imposed upon herself as much as on her victims. She considered herself a model of discretion—as indeed she was, compared with the fast women of society—and in this case never consciously intended a flirtation at all, but day by day yielded to the pleasantness of the moment.—By far the commoner case; for one woman who deliberately intends to do wrong, there are nine hundred and ninety-nine who drift heedlessly into equivocal situations.

The moment, too, at which her new friend had appeared had been unpropitious. She had been trying hard for a long while to be very good; to make the best of an unpromising state of things, to behave well to an unresponsive husband, to occupy herself with her books, her garden, and so forth. At first it had been all very well; but after a time she woke to find herself dead sick of it all. She wanted amusement, she wanted companionship more stimulating than that of Jenifer and Rachel. It was not mere love of admiration, but a hunger for something her life failed to give her, and a need for something or somebody to make much of. When Alick first returned, his suffering state appealed to that pitiful tenderness with which Nature had so richly endowed her, and gave her an excuse to enter upon more intimate relations than she might otherwise have done.

She had liked him from the first; she liked his looks, his height, his strong, sunburnt face, and the curious sea-shining in his eyes that sailors so often have, and the peculiarly mellow tones of his voice vibrated on her ear with an irresistible pleasantness. In character, too, he was such a contrast to the London men she had been chiefly thrown with, that he interested her. His very ignorance of many things with which she was familiar, refreshed her, backed as it was with brains and capacity enough in his own department of practical living; and she felt the subtle pleasure of being able to draw out a reserved and silent man whom others found it difficult to get on with. If a qualm ever seized her that she was letting their friendship grow to unmanageable lengths, she silenced it with the assurance that it had done her all the good in the world by taking her out of herself, and she was not going to throw it away at Mrs. Grundy's bidding. Moreover, she told herself that Alick Studland was pre-eminently a man to be trusted. In this she was perfectly right; he was the last man in the world to walk with his eyes open into an entanglement of this kind; the sort of thing had never been in his line at all; but possibly in a certain sense the risk was the greater from his inexperience in any such dilemma. As Rachel said, the fault was chiefly Letty's; it was she who had taken the initiative; but he would have been more than human if the subtle flattery of the preference of such a woman had not gone to his head.

They floated softly on, Alick pulling an occasional lazy stroke or two, but for the most part letting the current bear them along. They had not reached Letty's fanciful goal—never would reach it. The flickering, glittering mass with its hovering attendants had moved further westward, and they kept along under the cliffs, which to-day, instead of frowning darkly, were glowing with purple and red under the westering sun.

They talked a little lazily; that easy, fragmentary talk that two people enjoy who understand each other at the half word, or without the intervention of words at all. Now and then they sank into a dreamy silence, only broken by an occasional murmur from Letty, expressive of an absolute content. She would not take the trouble to steer, but let him scull, throwing a glance from time to time over his shoulder. Presently she became aware that the boat's head was going round, and she raised a protest.

"Oh not yet, not yet. We have hardly come any distance. Tea won't be ready for ages. Let us have another half-hour."

"Well," dubiously; "but you must remember how far the tide has brought us."

"It has been very obliging, hasn't it. You have had hardly any work. Don't be lazy; this is too delicious to be cut short."

"You don't suppose I want to get back?" he said. "I am happy enough."

There was an odd intonation in his voice. He leaned forward and looked into her eyes, and his look was like a caress. Letty wished she had not spoken; but the boat's head was round again now, and they sped on with a few strong strokes. He did not again propose to turn back till she herself reluctantly said—

"Well, it is a thousand pities, but everything nice must come to an end; I suppose we really ought to be getting back. Besides"—more prosaically—"I want my tea."

"Alick," she said presently, "don't you think you had better row a little harder? We don't seem to be making any way. Don't you notice we have been in a line with that cave for an enormous time."

He straightened himself for a moment, and wiped the drops off his forehead.

"I see," he said. "I am doing my best. I ought to have known what these currents are, but I reckoned on the muscles I used to have before my accident."

He bent to the oars again, for the boat had lost ground even in that momentary pause, and for every foot lost, it seemed to take an age to regain one painful inch.

"Oh, it was my fault!" cried Letty. "I ought not to have made you go on."

"You did not know. You see, it is so fatally easy to drift down the current; one forgets what it will cost to get back."

Letty was silent, aware that to waste his breath by making him talk would be no kindness; but she watched him distressfully, seeing the veins swell and stand out in knots on his forehead, and the muscles of his arms grow tense with strain.

At last she ventured on a suggestion.

"Isn't there any place where we could land and get up over the cliff?"

"A goat could; scarcely a man; certainly not a woman."

So she held her peace once more, and the little boat crept painfully back by the way she had erst floated so easily, and at length Gooseburn Cove came in sight. The golden glow had deepened through rose to greyness before they touched the beach, and the picnic party could be seen in the attitude of waiting with baskets packed and wraps on their arms, while the carriages might be decried in the lane above. It was not altogether a pleasant thing to have to land, and encounter all the questions, remarks, and reproaches that were directed to them, but it had to be faced. Studland tried to make light of his exhaustion, but he was forced to sit down upon a rock to recover himself a little before ascending the beach to where the horses were waiting. Mr. Jaques, who was walking on with the rest, came back.

"You are not fit to ride. I will take your horse and see Mrs. Dendron home. Your sister came in the Roscorla carriage, so you had better have a seat in mine, and John shall drive you up to Hennacombe as soon as he has set down the Wynnstays."

Alick tried to resist, but was too thoroughly done up for anything but submission, and Letty was subdued into consenting to any arrangement. They both felt they were being treated somewhat as though in disgrace. The miraculous appearance at this juncture of a cup of milk was a welcome distraction. It was Jenifer who, when it was decided that preparations must be made for an instant return on the reappearance of the truants, had saved the milk which some one was just going to give to the dogs, and had kept out a cup for them. She had slipped her supplies into Mr.

Jaques's hands before running on to take her place in the dog-cart.

Letty was a little in fear of her ride home with the vicar, but she need not have been; he was not given to meddling in other men's matters, and if he thought she had been imprudent, he forbore to say so. He was, however, rather a silent companion, and left her abundant leisure to meditate on her evil behaviour.

CHAPTER VI.

GRACE YEO was standing at the back door of the Vicarage taking a few minutes' rest before the kettle should boil. Behind her was the wide kitchen with its sanded floor, its black rafters, and its huge oaken table and settle, all in the perfection of afternoon order; before her lay the orchard in a flicker of sun and shadow. Down the steep, stony lane that ran between, came Peninah Sutton, stepping along with the easy carriage and fine pose of the head that distinguished her, a welcome sight to Grace, who did not often see a neighbour with whom to "change the weather, and pass the time of day."

"Good evenin', Mrs. Yeo," said the visitor. "I thought I'd step down along to knaw if ye'd care to have a couple of my ducklings, same as ye did last year. They're faine and plump."

Grace thought fit to be dubious.

"Well, I d'knaw whether or no I can du with'n. Measter, he'll be alone, and he d'not ate much poultry. But come your ways in," hospitably leading the way to the kitchen. "You'll lay off your hat, and stop to your tea? Us'll be losing our comp'ny next week."

"Iss, all the strangers is departing seemin'ly," said Peninah, accepting the invitation, nothing loth. "It have been quite a gay summer for the quality."

"Gay, indeed; rather tu gay, by all accounts." And Grace shook her head solemnly.

"Ah, so they du say. Faine gooins on up to Penquite."

"Ah, and wud ye believe now, he and she went off in a little boat together from the picnic down to Gooseburn, and never come back till near nightfall. John, he didn't get in till nigh upon eleven. He wud'n say much; 'twas the groom to Roscorla that told me. 'Twud'n surprise me nothin' if they meant to be off."

"Naw, you don't tell! Well, I wonder Pa'son don't spake to'n, that I du."

"Aw you see, t'measter's head is in the clouds, poor good man; he don't notice nothin'; but I du wonder what her husband is about."

"A poor silly fool; he lets her goo her awn way. He should give her a good clout on the head and shut her up till she come to her senses; that is what he should du. But Susy Cann—you mind Susy Cann? she used to live dairymaid with me when poor mother was alive, and she is housemaid up to Penquite now—she says he's a soft one. He sets there in his study, poking over's books, and so long as nobody meddles with him, he doesn't care what his wife does."

"Then he deserves all he gets, and serve him right. A woman don't think nothin' of a man who can't take his own part. I declare I'd sooner John knocked me about than left me to myself. But Susy Cann, she must have seen a dale?" and Grace looked inquisitively at her visitor.

"Well, there, I don't pay much heed to Susy Cann's havers; she always was the one to talk. 'That girl,' my poor mother often say—'she'd talk the hind leg off a donkey.' She did tell me once—— But there, I don't knaw as I'd ought to repeat it."

"Law, Miss Sutton, you knaw I wud'n goo for to make any mischief. Whatever did she tell?"

"Well, she du say he's hanging about there the whole blessed afternoon more days than not, playing and singing and one thing and another. 'Taint Susy's place to goo in the parlour—she wishes it was—a terrible curious girl is Susy — but the parlourmaid, when she took in the tea one day declares she believes he was a-kissin' of her. But there, we must remember that Susy Cann don't spake the treuth in general."

The caution was however lost upon Grace.

"Aw dear, and she a married woman! Shocking, shocking! 'Tisn't fittin'; and from them that did ought to know better, too. I never did have no opinion of them smart London ladies; but our own Mr. Alick, that was always so different. If it had been the young painter fellow from foreign parts, I shouldn't have been so surprised."

But Peninah bristled up in defence of her lodger.

"If you mean my young gentleman, Mrs. Yeo, I beg you won't name him in the same day with such carryin's on. A quieter, more decent livin' young gentleman doesn't breathe, be he foreigner or be he home-born. I wud'n have had him in my house if he had been one o' your light-o'-loves."

"No, Miss Sutton," said Grace, appeasingly; "to be sure you wud'n. And 'twud'n have been fittin' you should; you bein' such a personable woman for your years, and not that old neither."

"Well," said Peninah, rising, "I suppose I must be gooin' my ways home-along; the days is gettin' short. And when will I bring you down them ducks?"

Hardly had Peninah's tall form disappeared over the crest of the hill, than another visitor approached. Grace was clearing the table, but turned as a shadow fell across the open door.

"Why, Miss Jenifer," she cried, as she saw who it was, "you are quite a stranger! Were you looking for pa'son? He's just gone along to the church. Did'n you hear the bell. Mr. and Mrs. Wynnstay have driven over to Westcreek for the day."

"No, I didn't want Mr. Jaques, thank you, Grace. I came down this way to see if John was at leisure. I have got some new music I wanted him to try over. I thought he would just have finished the milking."

"So he have, miss; he brought me in the pails an hour ago; but at leisure he is not, for he haven't been in to his tea yet. He went off up the orchard. The gales is beginning, or soon will, and he thought he had better get in all them keddlestones before they was knocked all to pieces falling off the trees."

"It does not matter, thanks. I can leave the music for him. I was going on to Pencoet, and I thought I would call in as I passed."

"Aw, me dear, I wish you wud'n goo so often up to Penquite."

"Why?" asked Jenifer, quickly, and then wished she had not spoken; she could guess what Grace meant well enough, and on such a matter the least said the better.

"Well, there, I don't ha'f like to tell ye, But ye must ha' heard surely what all the folks is talking."

"Oh, I don't listen to all the talk in the village, Grace," said Jenifer, impatiently, "and I am surprised you should; I should have thought you had too much to do."

"Now don't ye be vexed with me, Miss Jenifer. Ah never was one to waste my time clacking, nor yet to lend my ear to no tales; but there's gooin's on up to Penquite that ye didn't ought to be mixed up in; 'tisn' fittin' for a young maid like you. There, I cud'n tell ye what Susy Cann have seen with her awn two eyes."

"I don't want to hear about it, thank you," and Jenifer turned resolutely away. "You mean kindly, I know, Grace, but it is a mistake to listen to all the exaggerated tales and gossip that gets about. Give John the music, please."

"If you want to spake to un yourself, miss, he's up the far side of the orchard. If you asts un, he'll tell ye 'tis every word treu, same as I have told ye."

As Jenifer went slowly up the orchard slope, she felt as if a weight had just been added to the scale in which she was balancing a resolution she had newly come to. It had nothing to do with it—absolutely nothing; but it deepened her conviction that the world was out of joint—at least her particular corner of it was—and she should like to get away and begin afresh somewhere else. She had not time for much consideration before she saw John's head appearing amidst the topmost laden boughs, like a very large black apple among the red ones. At the same moment he caught sight of her, and began to descend the ladder nimbly.

"There now, Miss Jenifer, to think you should have come down this afternoon of all others, and I should be that busy getting them apples. Us haven't had a practice I don't know when, what with faine comp'ny and the good weather for ploys and all."

"Never mind, John. I did not come to practice; I haven't brought my fiddle. I have got down some new trios, and I thought you would like to look them over; I have left them at the house for you. I mustn't hinder you; go on with your work."

"You'm not just well, be you, Miss Jenifer?" said John, eyeing her with some concern. "You'm leukin' like a ha'porth o' soap after a hard day's washin'. Do you think you cud ate an apple? Here's a real beauty. I'll wager you ha'n't got the like o' that up to Roscorla, have ye now?"

A homely consolation; but Jenifer accepted it in the spirit in which it was offered, and sat down between the russet and golden heaps on the ground to enjoy it at leisure.

"Oh yes, I am quite well," she said; "there is nothing the matter with me, only that I have a good deal to think of just now. Do you know, John, I believe I am going away."

"Going away, Miss Jenifer! Only just for a holiday like, you mane?"

"No, if I go, it will be my coming back that will be 'just for a holiday like.' But don't say anything about it, please; it isn't settled, and I have not mentioned it to any one yet."

John came down the few steps of the ladder he had re-ascended.

"I'll not say a word, miss, never fear. But wherever is it tu?"

"I hardly know that myself yet. But long ago Miss Treby said she could get me a post in a school, and I was silly and childish, and did not want to go; besides, they could not very well have spared me from home then; but now things are different, and I am going to her to-morrow, to ask if she can do anything for me now."

"A schule? But ye wud'n like that, Miss Jenifer. You that's always been used to have your awn way like."

"Have I? Well, perhaps it is time I learned not to have it."

The network of fine wrinkles deepened about John's keen bright eyes as he looked at her anxiously.

"Tell 'ee what it is, miss, you talk to pa'son about it. Don't you du nothin' hasty."

Jenifer had finished her apple, and rose from the grass.

"Well, I think I will take your advice. Good evening, John, and thank you."

As she got round to the front of the house, she saw the vicar, in cassock and trencher cap, coming down the path from the church, where he had been reading Evensong to empty pews, as his custom was. He had never been able to grasp the modern notion that the service is primarily for the edification of the worshippers. Old Mr. Treby once asked him if he thought it worth while. Septimus flashed round upon him. "Worth while! When I read prayers, I offer worship to God, not to the congregation." Nay, rather, he held that, in a scattered and hard-working parish, where few, if any, had the time to come and offer prayers for themselves, it lay the more on him to see that on his own part the rite was duly paid. Round all the uplying farm lands they would have missed the sound of the few strokes of Kerranstow bell, if it had been omitted, as if some regular natural phenomenon had suddenly ceased. Men set their watches by it, and timed the performance of their trivial duties.

"Why, Jenifer, have you come for some trios? Muriel will be in soon. We have all been terribly lazy about the music this summer weather. Why, where is the fiddle, eh?"

"No," said Jenifer, meeting him halfway, "I have not brought it. I came because I wanted to ask your advice."

"Come in then."

He led the way to the study, a long, low, book-lined room that under a woman's administration would have been the drawing-room.

"Now," he said, in his abrupt way, "what is it?"

"I have been thinking whether it would not be well for me, now Louisa is come back, to leave home, and be doing something for myself. I haven't said anything to my uncle and aunt yet about it; I wanted first to know what you would think."

"Leave home! You surprise me. Is anything the matter?"

"No, nothing is the matter; only I don't think they really want me now; that is all."

"Not jealous, eh? I should have thought there

was plenty of room for you both at Roscorla. Is it a case of a brawling woman in a wide house?"

"Oh no, indeed, not that; Louisa is most good-natured, and I don't think I am a brawler. We get on excellently. No, it is only that I am the fifth wheel to the coach."

"H'm." He took a turn across the long room and back, and then came and stood in front of her, his thumbs in the broad waistband of his cassock, looking at her as John Yeo had looked, only with sharper scrutiny.

"You are not happy, Jenifer; you are not yourself. What is it?"

His keen eyes drew hers like a magnet. She felt as if he were reading her very soul. She could not look away, but a flush rose in her cheeks. He turned away abruptly and coloured.

"I beg your pardon. I have no right to catechise you. I am forgetting that you are no longer a child. Well, now, tell me what it is you want to do."

It had flustered her a little, but she resumed steadily after a minute—

"Perhaps it is true that I have grown a little discontented, and yet I think it is wise that I should make a start for myself. You know I have very very little money of my own, and though my uncle gives me a home, I may some day have to work for myself. I remember long ago Miss Treby said how much wiser it would be if I were to begin now, while I am young and strong; only then they needed me at home, and I felt it would be ungrateful to go away; but now it is different, don't you see."

"I see. Perhaps you are right. Have you anything in prospect?"

"I don't quite know; only I heard Miss Treby say that the girl who took the situation she would have got for me two years ago, is going to be married, so I thought perhaps her friend would take me now. I am going to ask her; but I thought I ought to tell my uncle first, and I know he will only say it is nonsense, and not listen. If you would speak to him for me?"

"Well, well, we will see. But tell me more about it. What would you have to do? Where is it?"

"It is in Cheltenham, I believe; it is a boarding-house in connection with the ladies' college there. I should have to look after the girls, and take them to and fro to their classes, and mend their clothes, and help the younger ones prepare their lessons. I should have twenty pounds a year, and be able to attend some of the senior classes."

"Pshaw! A maid-servant would do as well."

"But you know I am not clever enough to be a governess. One needs so many certificates and diplomas and things nowadays to get anything at all."

He took another turn through the room, and then said—

"Has it never struck you, Jenifer, that that talent of yours was meant for something better than a plaything?"

She looked up eagerly. "You mean my music. But I have had so little teaching; what could I do?"

He drew a chair to her side and sat down. "Listen," he said, "I have a better plan than Miss Treby's. Would you like to go to Germany, and study music seriously?"

She grew pale, and her eyes shone.

"Oh, if it could be possible!"

"Well, I think it is a thing that not only can be but ought to be, now you are no longer tied at home, and I believe I see my way to it. Mrs. Wynnstay, who, as you know, is staying with me, has an aunt living in a place called Wimmelhahn, where there is a first-rate Conservatoire. She married a German officer, and is now left a widow with one daughter and small means, and Muriel thinks she would be glad to take in a young lady to board. I imagine that her terms would be moderate, and if your own little means are not sufficient, no doubt your uncle would help you for a time with the prospect of its rendering you independent. If you will allow me, I will myself gladly pay your first year's instruction at the Conservatoire. I expect by the end of that time you will have gained a scholarship, of which I am told there are a great many, and if not, why, then we will see. It will at any rate give you a start."

Jenifer held out both hands to him.

"How good you are! How am I to thank you?"

He took the hands and held them for a moment in his own firm, strong clasp.

"By working hard, and getting back your cheerfulness. There, don't say any more. I am thanked enough. I will come soon to Roscorla, and propose my plan to Mr. Lyon. You must stay and talk it all over with Muriel; she can tell you a great deal more about Wimmelhahn than I can. She and Hugh will be back at seven. We will have John in after dinner, and try over those trios, and you can use my Guarnerius. He shall put in the mare, and drive you home before they have time to get anxious about you."

CHAPTER VII.

"SO, my little maid, you want to leave us? Is that so?"

Old Mr. Lyon had just parted with the vicar at the gate of Roscorla, after listening to the latter's scheme for his niece's benefit, and instead of coming back to the house, had gone round to the farmyard. Jenifer had been watching in anxious impatience, and had hurried after him, loth to wait, and feeling that she would rather talk to him out-of-doors where they would not be interrupted. She joined him by the pigstye, where he was busy investigating the merits of a new litter. She slipped her hand into his arm.

"Dear uncle, you don't think me ungrateful? I think I ought to be doing something for myself; and though by what Mr. Jaques proposes I should not be earning yet, I should be preparing to do a great deal better than I could if I went out to a situation knowing no more than I do now. I think it is so very kind of him."

"So it is, so it is; but there is no need that I

can see. You have your home here, and always can have so long as I live, and though I ain't a rich man, you'll have your share of what I have to leave."

"Uncle, you have always been so good to me; but you have Louisa to think of."

"My dear, you have always done a daughter's part by me, and I shall see to it that you shall not come to want. Don't you be afraid."

"It was not that I was afraid of that; only I felt that I ought to be learning to do something for myself so as to be independent."

"There's no ought about it, my dear. There's your home here, and as much as you want to eat and drink; but if that don't content ye, I've no more to say. The little bit of money poor James left has most of it been laid by for you, except just what was wanted for your clothes and so forth, and I thought to go on putting it by till you were twenty-one. There should be a matter of fifty pounds a year or so by this time, so if you want it, take it and go to foreign parts with it, if that's what will please ye."

Active opposition would have been easier to meet. Jenifer sighed, and felt almost disposed to relinquish her cherished scheme. She said nothing, and Mr. Lyon began meditatively scratching the back of the old sow with a long stick, an attention which she seemed to appreciate greatly.

"I can't understand it," he went on presently. "There's something in the air seemingly, that makes all the young folks discontented, specially the girls. 'Tis natural for lads, to be sure; they must go out into the world and make their own way; but now the maids can't be content to bide at home, and live as their mothers did before them. Nowadays everybody has got a mission. Either they must write books or they must teach school, or they must play the fiddle."

"I don't know whether I have got a mission to play the fiddle," said Jenifer, with a smile, "but I do want to learn to do it really well instead of just wasting time over it as a mere amusement. I should like to work at it seriously, with the object of making it my profession. Don't you think it is good for a woman, as well as a man, to have some real work?"

"Ay, I suppose it is; you must be swimming against the stream, like living fish. Well, there, I see I must give in, and let you go."

"And you won't think it is because I am discontented at home?" said Jenifer, pleadingly; "for indeed I am not."

"Discontented? I could have understood that if it had been last year. It was lonesome for ye with only us old folks, but now you have got Louisa. Why, I was thinking she and you would be such company for each other."

"Yes; but then you see that will make all the difference to Aunt Martha; she could not have spared me if Louisa had not come home. I should never have said a word about going away while I felt I was of use; but now, you see, you won't miss me."

"Oh, you think not? Well, my dear, if your heart is set upon going, go; and when you are tired of your freak, there will be a warm corner for you at Roscorla — that is if I am above ground."

So the matter was settled, and it only remained for Jenifer to make her arrangements with Frau Klieschmann, and get ready her little outfit. For the latter object it was necessary that she should betake herself for a day's shopping to Bridesworth, since Kerranstow boasted but one small general shop, and Hennacombe was no better provided. Of course Louisa volunteered her company; a shopping expedition was just what she delighted in; but when the morning came, it found her a prisoner with a severe cold. Jenifer could not well put off; time would not allow, and secretly she was not very sorry to go alone, rather misdoubting whether she should have strength of mind to resist Mrs. Twisselton's advice and taste. Letty she knew would have gone with her; but just now she did not care to ask her.

She walked up to the cross-road at Craye to be picked up by the passing coach. Fred was apparently in a very bad temper.

"What an idiot you were, Jenny," was his greeting, as he helped her up to a seat at the back, where was the only vacant corner, "not to have sent me a postcard, and then I could have kept the box-seat for you. Now these cads have taken it, and I cannot well turn them out. You know there are always such crowds going back from Westcreek at this time of year, it is a wonder I have room for you at all."

Jenifer was not altogether sorry; she was not quite ready to encounter Fred and his objections yet. She was resolute in her purpose, but she was not quite without qualms. Except for a fortnight's visit to London under Mrs. Dendron's wing, she had scarcely been from home before, and it looked rather a fearsome undertaking to go to a foreign land all alone. Perhaps when all her purchases were made, she should be able to look on it more in the light of an accomplished fact, and reason about it as a thing from which there was no retreating.

If she expected her courage to rise at the end of the day, she was mistaken; she was tired out with dragging about from one shop to another. Whatever she particularly wanted seemed to be kept by some one at the top of the hill, or else across the river. Then she was discouraged by the friend with whom she had tea, who entertained her with stories of the shocking way in which young women who went abroad were liable to be taken in, and all the snares and pitfalls she would have to avoid. Moreover, Kerranstow gossip had contrived to travel these twenty miles, either by coach or brought by the legendary little bird, and she had to parry several annoying questions about

Mrs. Dendron. Altogether, as she stood on the pavement in front of the Golden Falcon, counting her packages as they were put in the coach, she felt weary and depressed, and in tune with the weather, which had turned cold and blustering.

She had not long to wait; Fred came out, buttoning his many-caped great-coat.

"Well, Jenny, up to time. You can have your pick of the coach pretty well now; not many passengers outward bound."

"If you don't mind," she said with a little shiver, "I would rather go inside; it has blown up so cold."

"Come now, that is not fair. I have not had a word with you, and I suppose I shall hardly see you again, if you are to be allowed to carry out your mad scheme. We'll wrap you up. Is that flimsy little jacket all you have got to put on across the moor? Here, Mrs. Widgett"—re-enter the hotel—"lend me a thick fur cloak or something for my cousin, will you? I'll bring it back with me to-morrow. Oh, never mind whether it is shabby; that doesn't signify so long as it is warm."

So Jenifer found herself perched on the box-seat, enveloped in a mountain of furs and shawls, lent by the good-natured landlady, and with a heavy waterproof apron tucked snugly beneath her feet.

"There, sit up close," said Fred, shaking the reins; "I shall keep the wind off you this side."

Then with a discordant too-tooing from Jem

Overend, the guard, they were off, the fresh horses breasting the steep ascent out of the town as if it were a mere molehill, and soon the wide river with its many-arched bridge, the grey church tower, and the old houses piled up one above the other, were beneath their feet, and they came out on the open moorland. They had been silent so far, Fred only addressing occasional objurgations to the horses; then he turned to look into her face.

"Jenny, what are you going away for?"

"You know I have always longed to study music really, seriously, and now that they have got Louisa at Roscorla there seemed a chance for me to get away, and Mr. Jaques found this opening for me at Wimmelhahn, so I suddenly made up my mind to it."

"H'm. I never thought you were one of the restless, ambitious sort. Can't you hit it off with Louisa? She always was a bit of a bully, but I should have thought you were very well able to hold your own."

Jenifer laughed. "It is very funny; everybody jumps to the conclusion that I can't get on at home. "It isn't that at all; but don't you understand the feeling of being superfluous? She does all the things I used to do, and I don't want to just drift along. I want a life of my own."

"Rubbish! What does a little girl like you want with a life of her own, as you call it—unless you mean a husband, and for that you need not go so far."

"Don't, Fred. You know I dislike that sort of talk."

"What was my uncle about to consent to your going off on such a wild-goose chase?" went on Fred, discontentedly. "As if Roscorla could possibly get on without you."

"Oh," she said, with a sigh that had a touch of bitterness about it, "Roscorla will do very well without me; I don't think any one wants me much."

"Don't they? I don't suppose you care whether I want you, or that you trouble your head about what is going to become of me when you are gone."

She got her hand with some difficulty out of her mufflers, and touched his softly.

"You know I do care; but what can I do? It is not my talking to you every now and then that can keep you straight. If you can't keep up for your own sake, and because you ought, it isn't likely that you will because a foolish little cousin lectures you whenever you are in the mind to be lectured."

"Ah well! It is no use saying anything. If you chose—but you know me a precious sight too well." He set his teeth hard.

Jenifer did not ask what he meant; she would much rather not know; but the conviction was forcing itself on her against her will. Till that moment no suspicion had ever entered her mind that his devoted affection for her could ever become other than cousinly. She had always regarded him as belonging to some one else, and that he should care for her in this sort of way disturbed her greatly. If, indeed, it were so, it was a reason the more for her going way. She held her peace, and so did he till they reached Tressider Cross, where they had to deposit the sole inside passenger.

On again over the broad desolate moor, with the strong south-westerly wind rushing to meet them, flawed now and again with a cold rain. Jenifer shivered, and he drew the wraps up round her, and tucked them in more securely about her feet.

"I suppose I have offended you, as you won't speak to me?" he said in a surly tone.

"Offended! Oh no; only surprised and puzzled me. I am so sorry if—but perhaps I did not quite understand you."

"No, I don't suppose you did; I am very far from understanding myself. I am not insulting you with the offer of such a worthless piece of goods as I am, with no money, no position, no reputation even. And I can't even promise you that if you took me I should be a reformed character; I don't suppose I should. I should have my ups and downs, same as I always have; and you are not like Katharine, you would break your heart over it. And yet I would do more for you— I always have done more at your bidding than for any creature on this earth. If you go away, there won't be a thing to hold me back."

"Oh, Fred, don't, don't!" cried Jenifer, distressed. "You have no right to put all the responsibility on me. I have always loved you as if you had been my brother, I always shall; but if I were to promise you any other sort of love, it wouldn't be real; it wouldn't do you any good. It is far better that I should go away; you will forget me. You forgot Katharine very quickly."

"I don't wonder you reproach me, but it is different; your little finger is more to me than her whole handsome person ever was."

"You can never have cared for her, then, as you pretended."

"Yes, I did, after a fashion; but there is more than one sort of caring, and that is what you women can never understand. Well, it is no use raking back into that; that is all over and done with. It was cursed ill-luck that ever made me talk to you so much about it; but you were a child then, and I little thought what was coming to me."

She did not answer; there seemed nothing to say; on such a subject it seemed useless to argue. She felt very wretched. It went to her heart to think that all the sympathy and help she had given her cousin had, after all, been only hurting him. Perhaps now, if he were disappointed in her, he would cease altogether from those upward struggles that had sometimes given her such hope for him. Ought she to forsake him? Since happiness was not for her, might she not sacrifice herself? Might she not do well to do the very thing Denis Kay had warned her against—give herself to save her cousin? If, as Denis fancied, she had loved him, it might have been worth the risk; but without a whole-hearted devotion she might as well try to save a drowning man with a thread of cotton. Dimly she perceived this; and, moreover, she had a saving conviction that to marry one man while there is another above ground whom, under other circumstances, one might, could, ought to have married, is to court disaster. She recalled her own words to him just now—"My love for you would not be real; it could not do you any good." She kept her head turned away from him as much as she could, but her hand went up to her face, and he bent forward and saw that she was crying.

"Darling," he said, "don't cry. I was a brute to have said anything. I did not mean to; I knew it would not be any good now. But look here," he went on, after a pause, "tell me one thing; supposing I were different; if I were the sort of fellow you could respect—if I went abroad, say, and made an entire fresh start, could you give me any hope?"

She felt as if she were murdering something as she answered—

"Oh, Fred, before all things, I must be honest. I could not."

He did not speak again, but lashed up the horses, and the coach rocked as they seemed to fly along the hard, level causeway. It was nearly dark now, and she could see the sparks fly out from the clattering hoofs. The clumps of gorse seemed to rush at them out of the darkness and go spinning past till she was almost giddy. She was not frightened; she had an absolute confidence in Fred's driving, and, besides, was in that mood when she would not have cared much whether anything happened or not. Presently she found, partly by the unusual bumping of the coach, partly by the dimly seen shapes of the hedges, that they had turned off the high-road into one of the lanes running down to Roscorla.

"Fred," she cried, "you are going wrong; you have turned out of the road."

"I know that. I am going to take you home. I don't choose to have you scudding all down that long lane from Craye by yourself. Besides, what are you going to do with your parcels, I should like to know?"

"Oh, I should have left them at the Kestrel till the morning, unless somebody met me with the trap. Very likely they will. I wish you would not come out of your way. You ought not, with the coach, really."

"Rot! There is nobody on it but you. I can go which way I choose, I suppose."

"I do wish you would not. There is such a horrid bit of road from Roscorla up to Craye. Do turn back."

"My dear child, their isn't room to turn a handbarrow here. Don't fuss."

She said no more, as they sped on, and in a few minutes the steaming horses were pulled suddenly up at the old stone gateway.

"Stand at their heads," cried Fred, in his imperious way, to the guard who came to the side to help her alight. He himself jumped down to lift her off the wheel, and helped her collect her parcels; then he stepped just inside the gateway, where the broad stone pillars shut off Jem Overend's view, and as she held out her hands for her packages, he flung them all down on the ground, and throwing his arms round her, held her close and kissed her repeatedly, before she quite knew what was happening. He had kissed her in old days often enough, but never like this, and it both frightened and angered her. As he loosed her, she stood for an instant breathless, unable to find words for her indignation. Then, as she saw how white and desperate he looked, her anger died on her tongue, and she only gave him a reproachful look, as she stooped to gather up her property.

"There, don't be furious," he said, as he turned away. "You have always been chary of your kisses. If I had asked for one, you would have refused me. It is the last time I shall ever kiss you."

A minute later she heard the coach go dashing up the lane, and Jem Overend blew an unearthly blast on his horn, lest any unwary traveller or belated haycart might be lingering in the road.

* * * * * *

"Beän't t'coäch coom in yet, then?" asked the landlord of the Kestrel, the wayside inn where the coach changed horses and where Kerranstow passengers were accustomed to alight.

"Naw, and a good job too, for them b'ys aint coom back from t'circus yet, and Jem, he do'an't like to play hostler. But t'is gettin' la'ate, surely?"

And Mrs. Dearlove stepped out to the door, tucking her arms under her apron, for the evening was cold.

"La'ate! Ah believe t'is la'ate. Her'd ought to ha' ben here an hour ago or more."

"And I made sure I heard the horn too, before ever I went to do the milkin', and I bade Sally carl to me so soon as ever they was in sight. Wherever can she be?"

The landlord stood out in the middle of the road, straining his eyes down the long straight line, still gleaming white between the hedges for a good distance, till the dusk swallowed it up; but the dark mystery at the end gave up no coach for all his gazing, only presently the solitary figure of a bent old labourer, with a fork over his bowed shoulders, shambling slowly along.

"Hullo!" cried the landlord as soon as the wayfarer got within earshot, "hev ye seen nought o' t' coäch, Meäster Pennyways? Her'd ought to ha' got here afore now."

"T'coäch, is it, Meäster Dearlove? Why her coomed along pretty nigh two hours ago. Her'd be ha'afway to Westcreek by now."

"Why, I tell you, man, she a'nt got here."

"What's gone wi' her, then?"

"That's just what ah want to knaw. Where was you when you saw her?"

"Up to t'long potater patch beyond Greenaways. Drivin' like the devil, they was. Fred Lyon was droonk, droonk as a lard."

"Not he," said Dearlove, with conviction. "Never drunk on t'road since ah've knawed un— and never sober off it. Tell ee what it is; ah'll take a lantern and goo up t'road a bit. Will ee coom? My lads is off to Widcombe."

"Naw, ah mun get home-along. Ah ben the length o' that road, ah tell ee. Ye won't find nawthin'." And he shouldered his fork and once more trudged on his way.

While her husband tramped off up the road with his lantern, Mrs. Dearlove went indoors, poked up the already noble fire to a blaze, and popped a knowing-looking little pointed saucepan into the hottest corner.

"Mr. Fred'll want his hot grog more'n ever if so be as they've got hindered, she said to herself. "I expect one of the horses cast a shoe, and that old idiot, Pennyways passed 'em by at the forge without ever seein' of 'em."

But she went out to the door again, and stood watching anxiously for the spark of her husband's returning lantern. She saw it presently, bobbing along and getting larger and larger. But he was alone. She ran out into the road to meet him.

"Ca'an't see naught of un. T'is a queer business, Prue. Ah went so far as the corner of Green Lane, too."

"Green Lane! you stupid, doan't ye see? Of course Mr. Fred must have gone down by Green Lane to Roscorla. Why ever didn't ye goo little-ways down and see."

"He wud'n goo to Roscorla. What for should he?"

"Why, Miss Lyon come up here this mornin' on purpose for to goo into Bridesworth with him. You may depend he wud'n have for her to goo back alone. He thinks a sight of his cousin, I can tell ee."

"Naw, he cud'n do that. Ah tell ee t'coäch must goo on, will he nill he. Why, there's parcels waitin' for un up to our house, and Lord knaws how many folk standin' by the wayside a'waitin' for to be took into Westcreek."

"Well, there wud'n be many such a night as this, if they was o' my way o' thinking'. But for dear sakes, take the lantern and goo down by Roscorla Bottom. My mind misgives me."

"Bless the woman! no man in his senses wud try to drive a coach round that way; but I suppose ah must take a look just to pacify ye." And grumbling, he set off once more.

"And a fool's errant ah be after, surely," he growled to himself, as he made his way along the steep, stony, ill-kept lane which ran by the combe-side, and connected the farm with the high-road.

"As if a lad like Fred Lyon, with a head on his shoulders, and knawin' right well what was due to his horses—no man better—wud ever ha' brought un down here. But ah might so well traipse the whole way while ah be about it."

A few yards further on, it struck him that the hedge did not look right; its usual outline seemed altered. He turned on his lantern, and saw that hedge, bank, and bushes were broken down—swept away, as though a torrent had dashed through them. He ran forward, sending his voice before him, and began to clamber down the steep descent, stumbling over the low bushes and stumps with which it was densely covered. Then he paused, for he thought he heard a voice from below.

"Be any one doon there?" he cried.

"Iss, but ah ca'an't move. Ah be main hurt. Us have had a overturn."

"So ye have, seemin'ly."

Guided by the voice, Dearlove had almost reached the bottom, and the uncertain light he held showed him a strange wreck. The coach lay on its side, one wheel left in the bushes above, another trundled down into the brook below; splinters of shaft, smashed panels and bits of broken harness lay scattered in every direction, and it was a minute before, amidst the *débris* he could discover Jem Overend under the bulky shadow of a horse. Another lay groaning its life away a few yards lower down.

"He's dead, this poor brute," said Jem, "and ah

ca'an't get my leg away from under'n. Cud'n ye help me a bit? Aw dear!"

Setting his lantern on the ground, Dearlove succeeded in freeing the unfortunate man, who crawled out, a sorry spectacle, bruised and scratched, and white with terror and pain.

"Her's broke, ah du think," he said, feeling the leg on which the horse's weight had lain. "And however be I tu get up the bank?"

"But where's Mr. Lyon, then?" asked Dearlove, stumbling round among the ruins.

"Ah d'knaw. He must ha' gone after them other two horses; they broke traces, and galloped clean away. He d'always think more of the beasts than o' human critturs. Ah was stooned like at the first, and when ah coom to myself, ah carled to un and carled to un, but ah cud'n make him hear."

"And the passengers, poor souls?" pursued Dearlove, trying to peer through the pit of the broken window.

"There were'n't none, thank the Lard. Though ef there had a ben we should never have coom down this cursed place. Eh! have you found un?"

"Good God!"

"What, dead?"

"Ay, dead, and pretty nigh cold. Poor chap, poor chap, t'was all over with him soon enough. He's layin' with his head on a big stone, ha'af in the brook."

"Let me get to un. Help me doon, wull ee."

And Jem began to crawl down the bank, regardless of the agony in his broken limb.

"You bide where you be. You cud'n do un no good, ah tell ee. He'll never spake no moor."

And, hearing that, the rough fellow lifted up his voice and wept.

CHAPTER VIII.

SEPTIMUS JAQUES and his old white horse were jogging slowly along, past Peninah Sutton's. As he reached the gate, he drew rein, remembering that he had promised Grace to call and leave word about some honey the next time that he should find himself in that direction. He called out, not caring to dismount, but it was not Peninah who came in answer to his summons, but the painter, in his grey linen blouse, palette on thumb, looking as though he had never gone away.

"Hullo, parson, it is awfully good of you to come up so soon to see me. How did you know I was back? Come in, come in. You know your way to my studio. I'll take your horse round, and find Ebenezer to put him up."

Septimus was rather embarrassed at this cordial reception. He was a man who felt likings and dislikings very keenly, and showed them very plainly, and at this moment his former favourite was decidedly in his black books.

"Thanks," he said, somewhat shortly. "I did not come to stop; merely to leave a message with Peninah, if she is within. I am afraid I must confess to not having known that you were expected."

Kay felt a little rebuffed; but, innocent of any possible cause of difference, rejoined—

"But, surely, since I am here, you won't go away without coming in. I have a bit of work on my easel that I should like your opinion on. It is a thing I began last March, and I found, to finish it satisfactorily, I must have a week here when the autumn ploughing begins. In fact, that is what has brought me down again."

It was impossible without absolute discourtesy to refuse this invitation, so Mr. Jaques slowly dismounted, and having given old Blanche into the care of Ebenezer, Peninah's man-of-all-work, followed Denis into the studio. On the big easel, under the skylight, stood a large unfinished canvas. A solitary ploughman at work on one of those little sloping, triangular scraps of field, clinging to the cliff side, that look as though they could never repay the labourer for his toil. Above, it was divided by a hedge of brambles from the sweep of barren moor; below, the hungry sea was gnawing at the rocks. Sky and sea were grey alike, with cold March greyness that seems to steal all richness even from the brown earth.

The two men stood by it for a minute, neither feeling very ready to begin a conversation, till Mr. Jaques said—

"That is a powerful bit of work; but it is very depressing."

"I suppose it is. I am afraid it will not be very popular. I thought it so depressing myself that I had laid it aside, and then the fancy took me to finish it, and I found I wanted some more details of the plough; the surroundings, of course, I shall not touch again; the time of year being so different; but I thought there might be ploughing going on again by now."

"But, surely," said the visitor, "you need not have come all this way to see a plough at work. Such things may be found nearer than Kerranstow."

Kay laughed. "True; but I wanted the feeling of the place—that intangible something without which I can do nothing worth doing. Besides, I—well there, it does not matter. But do you know, you speak rather as if you resented my coming down. Have I been so unfortunate as to offend you?"

He looked his visitor straight in the face; the two pairs of keen eyes met and crossed like the pass of a rapier.

"Offend me? Certainly not. It is no affair of mine; I have no quarrel with you. At the same time, I have my own opinion. It is a matter which no doubt in your world you think little of; still, if you find a less hearty reception at Kerranstow than you used to receive, you will probably understand well enough to what to attribute it."

"Upon my soul I don't," said Kay. "I am quite at a loss to imagine what you are referring to. I wish you would be a little more explicit. If you have heard anything to my discredit, I beg you will speak out, and give me a chance to defend myself."

"I have heard no reports about you whatever. It is simply a matter of my own observation, and one on which least said the better. I should not have mentioned it, had you not taxed me with a want of cordiality. I am sorry to have been forced to say so much. I will wish you good day."

He took up his hat, and moved towards the door.

"Under these circumstances I cannot wish to detain you," said Kay, with dignity; "but I think you are under some mistake which I hope may be cleared up some day."

As they reached the outer door, it appeared, however, that Mr. Jaques was not to make his escape quite so easily. During the few minutes that he had been in the house, a heavy black cloud that had been threatening for some time, had begun to discharge the first big drops, and a vivid flash of lightning warned him what was to be expected. For himself, perhaps, he would have braved it, but a merciful man is merciful to his beast, and Blanche hated thunder and lightning.

"You cannot start in this storm," said Kay, with cold politeness. "You must accept the shelter of my roof till it is over."

"Thank you," said the vicar a little stiffly, "on condition you will not let me interrupt your work."

So Kay took up his brushes again, not sorry to be occupied, for the situation was a little strained. Mr. Jaques, who had said more than he intended, hardly knew how to resume the conversation; but the painter, who was seldom at a loss, presently said—

"I was so shocked to hear of the accident to the coach the other day. What a ghastly business it must have been. But I cannot understand it at all. How came the coach off the high-road? Did the horses bolt, or what? From the newspaper account, it seems to have happened at Roscorla Bottom."

"Why, it seems poor Lyon thought fit to drive round by Roscorla to set down his cousin who had been in to Bridesworth for the day. There were no other passengers the last half of the way, and I suppose he thought he could trust to his admirable driving, and wanted to save her the walk down from the inn. She declares he was perfectly sober, but Jem Overend, the guard, says 'he was driving like the very devil,' and when something startled the horses—an owl, Jem thinks it was—he lost control, and they swerved and dashed over the low hedge before he could get them in hand. It was a mercy she escaped; he had not set her down five minutes."

Kay stooped to work intently on a brown clod in the foreground while he asked—

"How did she bear it?"

Mr. Jaques gave him one of his quick, fierce looks, as much as to say, "What is that to you?" Aloud he said—

"She was naturally very much distressed; she was always very fond of her cousin."

"Ah!" said Kay, softly, still intent on his work; "I was afraid so."

"Afraid so? What do you mean?"

As he spoke, Septimus sprang up from his distant chair, and came round to the window.

"I was afraid there was an attachment, and he—not to speak evil of the dead—was never worthy of her."

"You are entirely mistaken; there never was anything of the kind. Why, he was engaged till quite recently to a young lady in Bodmin."

"I know; but still—and that has been broken off."

"So! Why, if that was what you got in your head——" He stopped abruptly, it was a sentence difficult to finish; but Kay was a man of quick intuitions; his mind flew like a woman's from point to point, and in a moment he saw the whole thought of the other quite as clearly as if it had been put into words. He laid down his palette and smiled.

"I see. I know now why you thought you ought to hate me. One doesn't exactly care to publish one's own defeat; but I think I owe it to myself, and in a certain sense to her too, to tell you that I proposed to Miss Lyon months ago, and she refused me. I should have done so long before if I had had any encouragement. You thought I was trifling with her?"

"I did; I confess it. My dear fellow, forgive me for jumping to such unwarrantable conclusions. I am distressed."

"Never mind. I should have deserved a good deal worse at your hands if I had really been such a cad. Only I can't quite forgive you for spiriting her away. However, I suppose it is all for the best. It would have been too soon. I must bide my time."

"You don't give up hope, then?"

Kay made no answer to that, but took up his brushes again.

"I am afraid I have been a meddlesome old fool," said the vicar, restlessly swinging the blind-tassel. "You see, I have known her from a baby; I don't think I could feel more for her if she had been a child of my own; it roused all my indignation to think she had been dealt with unfairly."

"I wonder what put the notion into your head."

"Well, it was natural, after seeing your very evident preference, to expect the usual conclusion; and when, instead of that, I saw her drooping more and more as the summer went by, and you kept away, and then when she came to me, restless and unhappy, longing to get away from home, and throw herself into some active occupation, with the instinct of a healthy mind ill at ease, as I thought, what could I suppose? I thought she was taking the best means to fight her trouble, and I gave her what help I could."

"And you thought I was such a cur as to have made her love me, and then left her without a word? That was hardly fair."

"I own it. I thought you were probably not aware of the mischief you had done. You are an ambitious man, Denis, and she has neither money nor position to attract such an one."

"I am ambitious; but not of climbing by a woman's hand. I am grieved at what you tell me about her; it confirms my own idea. But now the poor fellow is dead, she will get over it."

The vicar laid his hand on the other's shoulder.

"I hope you will win her yet, Denis. I could not wish better for her. I used to think what a good thing it would be if she and Studland were to make a match of it, but now——"

"Ah," said Kay, "I have been hearing some rather queer reports; but my good Peninah has rather a long tongue, I did not pay much heed. Is there anything really amiss?"

"I wish I knew. I don't know what to think. There is great imprudence at the best, and it is causing a talk which is bad every way. One tries to shut one's ears to gossip, but there comes a point when a thing of this sort should be either sifted or put an end to in some way. Did Peninah give you the idea of a serious scandal?"

Kay shrugged his shoulders.

"Those sort of people always put the worst constructions," he said. "I own I was astonished. Studland would have struck me as the most unlikely man to get into a scrape with a married woman. But there is no accounting for these sort of things."

Septimus took a restless turn or two up and down the room.

"But what ought I to do?" he said half to himself.

Denis looked up from his painting.

"I doubt the wisdom of interference in such cases," he said; "it sometimes brings on a crisis."

"Ay; but should I do nothing if they were in a different station? If a warning could prevent mischief—Heaven knows I hate the notion of interfering. Well, the storm is over; there is a gleam of blue sky. I must be off."

And he was gone almost before Kay had time to realize his intention.

Halfway home he passed Rachel Treby walking. She made as though she would have stopped to speak, and he instantly dismounted.

"You looked as if you had something to say to me," he said in explanation, as she stood silent, after responding to his greeting, pushing little pebbles diligently into a puddle with the point of her umbrella.

"I hardly know whether I had or not. I am puzzled," she answered.

It was a new thing for Rachel to suffer from any

kind of uncertainty; she who was always so clear as to her own duty as well as other people's. He slipped his arm through Blanche's rein.

"Come," he said, "we are going the same way; let us stroll on together, and if there is anything you wanted to speak of, you can think it over."

With her opportunity so clear and plain before her, Rachel could hesitate no longer. She took her courage in both hands.

"It is about my step-brother and Mrs. Dendron. I don't wish to say one word to spread reports further; but you must have heard what people are saying about them, and it seems to me it has got to a point when something ought to be done. I can do nothing with Alick, and my father—well, you know what my father is."

He walked on silently beside her for several yards.

"Miss Treby, this is an awkward matter to interfere in."

"Awkward!" Rachel's ready indignation blazed out. "Is that all you think of it? I did hope you would realize the scandal of it, and all the harm it is doing. When it gets to the poor people talking of it as you know they do talk—saying the most dreadful things—surely it is time that some one interfered. I think you might speak to them."

Mr. Jaques stood still. If he had had any suspicion of the topic of Rachel's discourse, he would rather have ridden off in the opposite direction than dismounted to lend an ear to it.

Shyness and his rooted objection to feminine dictation alike counselled flight. He put his foot in the stirrup.

"I do not think any good end would be served by our discussing the subject," he said, with his head over his shoulder. "It is one that is very much on my own mind. Good morning."

And Blanche disappeared down the lane at a pace considerably quicker than her usual sedate amble, leaving Rachel half amused at his abrupt flight, wholly indignant both with him and with herself.

"I might have known it would be as much use to consult the Shag," she said to herself, as she walked on. "I am sometimes tempted to think that men have no moral sense."

Septimus Jaques had great faith in the efficacy of manual labour as an antidote to worry. In the afternoon he betook himself to the carpenter's shop which he had set up in a disused apple-loft. Jacquot came too, and walked about on the workbench among the shavings, watching his master, with his head very much on one side. There was a panel missing in the rood-screen, and the vicar, who was an accomplished woodcarver, meant to try and replace it himself, without meddling with the old work, having a wholesome dread of getting into the ruthless hands of the professional restorer. John Yeo was at work at the other end of the bench, shaping a bit of old oak for the moulding.

"This is a sad business about Temperance Polsue,

John," said the vicar, presently, when the noise of the saw ceased for a minute, as he laid down the broad black pencil with which he had been tracing out his pattern, and took up his chisel.

"T'is so, sir. I met them a'taking of her in to the Workhouse this morning early. Crying she was, poor soul, fit to break her heart. A turrible firm man is Jeremiah."

"Ah, poor thing. Well, we must see what can be done for her, by-and-by, that she may not go from bad to worse. I am bitterly disappointed. A family that has always been so respected in the parish, and held their heads so high. It is all very well for Jeremiah to show sternness now, but he should have taken better heed to his daughter. I was in hopes there was getting to be a higher tone of feeling in such matters."

"Graäce takes it to heart sorely," went on John. "Never such a thing happened in the fam'ly before. She can't hold up her head hardly to hear talk of it. T'is a sore disgrace. But there! what can ye expect when there's such carryin's on amongst the quality?"

John was accustomed to use considerable freedom of speech to his master unrebuked; the relation between them was no common one.

"I can't affect to misunderstand you, John; but the cases are not parallel."

"Maybe so, sir; but them two has made themselves the talk of the parish from the one end to the other."

"Talk! Ay, there has been enough and to spare of that, and it only makes things worse. You know me well enough, John, to know that I should not excuse in one class what I should condemn in another; but there may be folly, frivolity, indiscretion that fall far short of actual wrong-doing. Understand me, I condemn it utterly, but I condemn no less the spirit that puts such talk abroad and keeps it going."

He bent to his work again, and John held his peace; the room was silent but for the scrooping of the saw, and Jacquot's remarks, as he threw curled shavings over his back and stalked about with them trailing behind him, like a child playing at being a fine lady in a train. It was comical enough, but neither master or man were in a mood to observe his antics. Presently there was a tap on the door, and Grace put in her head.

"Mr. Dendron to see you, sir."

Mr. Jaques resumed his coat—he had been working in his shirt-sleeves—and went downstairs. The day had turned cold since the storm, and Grace had lighted a fire in the study. Oliver was sitting by it, holding out his chilly white hands to the blaze; a grave, dull-looking figure, with the formal whiskers that gave him such an old-fashioned air, just touched with grey.

"I came," he said, after the usual greetings had been exchanged, "to remind you of those slates. We had the rain into our attic again the night before last. It should be seen to before winter, I think."

"I am extremely sorry for the delay. I have written again to the quarry. You know they sent us machine-cut slates instead of rough. I don't think I could consent to disfigure Pencoet with a patch of smooth blue slate."

"Indeed no. Mrs. Dendron would be the first to cry out upon such a deed of vandalism. We must wait. I merely thought I would call and make sure it had not slipped your memory."

He began to pick up hat and gloves; he seemed to have no more to say. What a difficult man he was to talk to! was the vicar's reflection. Rising as the other rose, he expressed a hope that his tenants were comfortable and likely to remain.

"Oh I hope so, I think so; yes. But that reminds me to ask you; supposing I did wish to sub-let—there is another year of our three years' term to run, you know—should you have any objection?"

"Certainly not, to a careful and satisfactory tenant; but are you thinking of leaving?"

"No, I don't wish to do so; but it might happen." He laid down his hat again, and put his gloves very carefully inside it. "The fact is, I have been made very uneasy, and I cannot tell what it might be best to do."

No answer was possible to this, but an indistinct murmur of regret. Mr. Dendron stared into the fire for some moments, then resumed—

"I met with a neighbour yesterday. It is perhaps wisest not to mention names—and she took upon herself to give me some most unpleasant, and I may say most impertinent hints on the subject of—of a visitor Mrs. Dendron is in the habit of receiving. I should have thought little of it, but for some remarks I accidentally and most unwillingly overheard from the servants." He stopped; he seemed to have great difficulty in expressing himself; then, looking the other straight in the face, he burst out suddenly, "Tell me, is there anything in it?"

"You mean, is it a fact that gossip has arisen on the subject? I am afraid it is so. In a country place remarks are very soon made, and it is for you to consider whether it were not well that it should not be allowed to go further. I don't wish to appear intrusive, but since you have yourself mentioned the matter to me, I cannot help saying that, however little foundation there may be, such a thing is never harmless to a woman. I think you should remember that the persons concerned are the last who ever hear what people are saying about them. Probably a hint to Mrs. Dendron would be quite sufficient."

Oliver made a slight gesture of despair.

"I don't know what to do," he said; "I have always had the most entire confidence in Mrs. Dendron's discretion. I shrink from taking her to task, or appearing to suppose there could be any occasion; in fact, I can't do it. I don't know whether you will understand me, but I have the feeling that it would be taking a step from which there would be no receding; that if I am unjust, she could never forgive me, and if I am not——" He stopped, and his lips went white. In a moment he recovered himself, and went on, "We have never had a quarrel since we married."

Mr. Jaques could not help thinking that even a quarrel might be a wholesomer condition than this cold, slow estrangement. Then he said—

"Would it not perhaps be wise to break off present entanglements by a short absence, a little trip abroad, or something of that kind? It is fair to recollect that this dull country life may be very trying to a bright, attractive young woman."

"Very true. I ought to have thought more of that in the first place, but she seemed to accommodate herself to it so charmingly; and now I hardly know—for one thing I am extremely reluctant to take flight; it seems to admit too much. Then if his pursuit is serious, what is to hinder him following us? And abroad the case would be worse; I cannot act as a spy upon her."

He rose, and went and leaned on the chimney-piece, his head on his hand.

"I am exceedingly unhappy," he said.

The words sounded formal, but they betrayed a very bitter grief. Septimus rose too, and went nearer.

"You need not be; I feel sure you need not be," he said. "I believe nothing but idleness is at the root of it all. They have been imprudent, and forgotten appearances, which in this wicked world of ours have to be considered; but I have known Alick Studland all his life; he is the last man in the world to act in an unprincipled way. Do not take it tragically; it will only make matters worse."

"Perhaps I am making too much of it; I trust so"—with an effort to recover his ordinary demeanour. "I hope you are right. I have not been feeling well lately, and when that is the case things are apt to look black. I feel I have not made allowance enough for her youth and love of pleasure. I thought I was doing the best for her in leaving her entirely free to pursue her own amusements; but it seems to have gone all wrong."

"Freedom to follow her own devices might be all very well," said the vicar. I am an old bachelor, and have no right to an opinion—probably you will tell me I am sentimental; but it seems to me a woman wants something more than that to secure her happiness. What about loving and cherishing?"

"Ah, if she would have let me—I don't know whose fault it was; I thought it was going to be very different. I am afraid I did not understand her; she was so unlike the women I had been used to. She was so young-looking, so soft and gentle, I thought it would have been an easy task to mould her to my own views. I might as well have tried to mould running water. My mother always warned me we were not suited, but I thought if only I could win her, all would be well. And God gave me my desire, and sent leanness withal into my soul. It is because I know I have not her heart that I have no security."

"Well, I will give you one more piece of advice. You say you have been feeling ill; go home and tell her so, and enlist her sympathy. It will do you more good with her than a hundred reproaches."

He shook his head. "I have never troubled her with my ailments. I can't begin; especially just now, when we seem more aloof than ever. Well, I must go. I am thoroughly ashamed of the way I have been talking about myself; I never did such a thing before in my life; but it has been a very great relief. I think I get morbid sometimes."

He shook hands, and his hand had more of a human grasp in it than it had ever had before.

When he was gone, Septimus took several quarterdeck turns up and down his study.

"Poor fellow, poor fellow; I wish I knew what to do. What a fool the man is, to be sure. If mischief does not come, it will be no thanks to him. Those two do not intend to go wrong, I maintain it; but who knows when the current may not gain strength to sweep them both away?"

He took his hat, and went out upon the cliff.

CHAPTER IX.

ALICK STUDLAND had taken his gun, and strolled through the furze and bracken with some vague intention of potting rabbits, but so far he had not wrought much havoc. He had begun to feel the need of some excuse, less to others than to himself, for going so constantly in one direction; but his misgivings were quite incoherent; he had avoided putting them into shape. He thought he would not call at Pencoet to-day; nevertheless, when five o'clock came, it occurred to him that it might do just as well to make for the shore at Pencoet Mouth. He was not wrong. There sat Letty with her back against a boulder, surrounded with her books, her knitting and her picnic kettle. She looked up with a smile of welcome, but no surprise, as her visitor descended.

"I thought I heard your gun," she said, "so I told Fanny to bring out a second cup, in case you found your way down here. I am glad you did not bring the poor little dead bunnies with you; I can't bear to see them."

He laughed. There aren't any. They are all alive and frisking up above. I missed them, you will be glad to hear. I don't know what is the matter with my eyes; all the little beggars made off and scoffed at me."

"You want your tea. It is just ready to pour out. I did not set light to the kettle till I saw you beginning to come down."

He lay down on a patch of soft sand at her feet, and watched her. It was growing chilly for sitting out-of-doors, and she had twisted a fur round her throat; her fair face and curly head came out of it like a delicate flower out of a rough calyx. He recalled incredulously the time when he did not think her pretty. Had he been blind, or had she changed? To most people the change in her would have seemed more loss than gain. She was not so brilliant as she had been; she had lost some of her youthful bloom; but there was more tenderness about her; there had come a little wistful droop about the corners of her mouth that touched him more closely. There was a great deal of pity mingled in the sentiment with which he regarded her.

It made her nervous to feel his eyes upon her so; she had ceased to feel as much at her ease in his company as she used to do, and she rattled the cups and saucers together in a way very unlike her usual deft-handedness.

"How cold it is!" she cried. "Oliver has actually been cowering over a fire this afternoon.

I tell him he wouldn't be so cold if he went out more, as I do; but, after all, I suppose the summer is over, and this about the end of our unconventional outdoor teas. Even in this sheltered nook it gets chilly."

"Ah, I suppose it must all come to an end soon now," he responded gloomily.

She tried to laugh. "Don't take that tragic tone," she said. "If we can't amuse ourselves out-of-doors, we must make the best of things by the fireside."

"I was not looking at it quite so literally. No, what I am thinking of is that I ought to have been gone long ago. I had no business to stay so long. I am nearly well now. What it means for me is that now summer is over, everything is over."

She looked down at him, and she knew she ought not to say it, but some reckless impulse moved her.

"Don't talk of it," she whispered, "I shall miss you so."

He half rose from his leaning posture. Her hand lay near him on the sand; he seized it and began to speak—rapidly, incoherently—what he scarcely knew, neither did Letty, but it startled her. She snatched her hand away, and sprang hurriedly to her feet.

"Mr. Studland," she said, "I am going in. Don't hurry to finish your tea; I shall send the servant down for the things later."

He rose too, and stood looking at her with dazed eyes.

"Forgive me. I will not offend again. After all, what have I done?"

"Done? nothing. Only made me repent of my friendliness."

"You are unjust," he began.

"Very likely. I don't choose to argue about it. Don't say anything more."

He obeyed her. Without further leave-taking he picked up his gun and went up the steep path that led over the Shag's Head. She busied herself collecting her knitting-needles and balls of wool till he was nearly out of sight; then she paused and looked after him.

"It was entirely my own fault," she said to herself. "I was rash and very silly; but, after all, I don't believe there is much harm done, or I should not have sent him off so easily. If he had been a different kind of man I should have been more on my guard, and I don't suppose I should have gone so near the edge of the permissible. I must be more careful. I will not, no, I will not be drawn into a scrape. But oh, how dull it will be when he is gone."

Breathless from something more than the climbing, Studland found himself on the summit of the cliff, where a broad level greensward stretched like a terrace for a hundred yards or so. It was such a favourite place with the vicar for an evening stroll, to watch the sunset, that the people had dubbed it "Parson's Walk." He was there now, his gaunt black figure standing out against the blue-green sea; rather an unwelcome sight to Alick, who wanted to get his thoughts a little in order, rather than talk to any one just now. There was no help for it, however; the two met midway.

"Ha, Alick, out with your gun? I am glad to see that. I hope it means that you are almost well again. Is the side quite healed up?"

"Quite, thanks. I have had no more trouble with it the last three weeks. It is a bit stiff and sore yet; that is all."

"Ah, you did it no good with that tremendous row the other day. You had no business to have attempted it; the only wonder was that it did not do you more serious damage."

"I suppose it was rather mad."

Alick spoke shortly; at this moment he did not want the imprudence of that row brought home to him.

Mr. Jaques wished he could lead naturally from this topic to the one on which it lay on his mind to speak; but somehow the opening did not seem feasible. He tried another route.

"I suppose, then, you will be leaving us soon now?"

The moment before Alick had been saying to himself that he really must go, and the sooner the better; but with the perversity ingrained in human nature, so soon as he perceived that some one else thought so too, he replied—

"I don't know. I am by no means fit for service yet. I think I shall apply for another month or six weeks at least."

"I am sorry to hear it. I know it sounds very uncivil, and if your leave had been just at an end, I would sooner have held my tongue; but I think you must be aware how very desirable it is that you should not be loafing about here longer just now. If you are wise, you will cut it short."

Studland set his teeth hard, and looked out over the wide emerald and purple streaks without seeing them. He did not want to answer hastily. If he could take censure at all, it would be from the man beside him, whom he had loved and respected all his life; but no man likes to be taken to task on a matter of personal conduct; least of all if he feels it is deserved. He was silent, and the other went on, speaking rapidly, but with an effort.

"I don't think you realize the harm you are doing. I would be the last to think evil. I have watched and have held my peace; but every week seems to add to the mischief. I cannot let you go on without a word of warning."

"I will not pretend not to understand what you mean," said Alick, coldly. "Because I have visited pretty frequently at a house where the hostess is young and pretty; because in this deadly lively place she and I have become a little more intimate than conventionality thinks necessary, every evil tongue in the parish is set wagging. I own I am surprised that you should listen to it; I did not think you were the man to kowtow to Mrs. Grundy."

"I am not doing anything of the kind," snapped out Mr. Jaques, whose temper was none of the smoothest, and who hated the task before him as only a shy man could hate it. "You think I am interfering in what does not concern me; but I tell you it does concern me. I am set over the souls in this parish, and I am answerable for them before God. I have striven all my life to stamp out the laxity and immorality that was rampant here when I came, and am I to see my work all undone because those who should set an example show instead an utter and selfish disregard of appearances? You may call it unconventionality; these country-folks do not discriminate; they call it by a harder name."

Alick flushed hotly. "You are making the most unwarrantable assumptions," he said.

"That may be. I hope it is so. I only speak of what I see, and that warrants me in warning you that you are going too far—very much too far. I cannot comprehend, for my part, how you could suffer the name of a woman for whom you have a regard to be dragged down in common talk, as hers has been through this. I can only suppose you were not aware of it."

"Of course I was not. Is it likely any one would dare to say such things to me? Could I suppose such scandal would be for a moment listened to or believed?"

"Well, now you do know, for Heaven's sake cut it short, before worse comes of it."

Alick drew a long breath. "I cannot be dictated to. It seems to me a monstrous thing," he went on, "that a woman situated as she is, married to a stick with whom she has not two ideas in common, is to be debarred from anything in the nature of a real friendship, because of the evil tongues of the world."

"That sounds very well and specious, but it won't hold water. It is precisely because of the lack of perfect understanding with her own husband that she will do well not to choose a young man for her friend. A woman happily married may make friends where and with whom she will; but I need not point out, when the friend grows dearer than the husband, what the end must be. I don't believe you have ever looked forward, or weighed the risks you are running, so, at the price of your anger, I have warned you, as I would have warned you had I seen you walking over that cliff yonder with your head over your shoulder."

"I know you mean it kindly, but I cannot admit the necessity. I am not a boy, and I hope I have some grains of sense and self-control."

"Ay, but, Alick, one's own case is always an exception. Just look at it as you would have done if it had been anybody else. She is a most attractive creature, and a man must have great confidence in himself if he can be sure he might not be beguiled without meaning it."

Alick faced round fiercely. "Take care what you say about her. Though she is no prude, no man would ever dare to overstep the line she chose to lay down."

"I like to hear you say that. I hate a man who says 'the woman tempted me.'"

"It is on her account I feel so furious," went on Studland, angrily; "that she should be held up to reprobation because she has permitted herself a little solace in her loneliness, in the company of a man who at least can appreciate her better than that selfish, indifferent brute, who never troubles his head what she does, or how she amuses herself, from one month's end to another."

"You are mistaken in him. They misunderstand each other, I grant; but there are faults on both sides. He is feeling it very deeply."

"Do you mean to say he complained to you about it? What an unutterable cad!"

"No such thing. I have given you quite a wrong impression, if you think he did anything of the kind. He came to me on a matter of business, and in the course of our talk he betrayed to me, almost involuntarily, some glimpse of the very great distress he was feeling at some disclosures that had been forced upon him. If he has erred, it has been from too much confidence in his wife, rather than too little. But I will say no more about that. I am not authorized to do so."

They paced along silently side by side for a few yards; then Studland broke out—

"Oh! the mischief of evil tongues; they are the very devil."

"True enough; and yet, Alick, they are not the whole mischief in a case like this. I am perhaps going beyond my province in touching upon the personal aspect of the question, but you and I are very old friends, and you will forgive me. It seems to me when two people slide into questionable relations, it is not the evil-mindedness of the lookers-on alone that signifies; the real danger lies nearer home; not so much in what they may say, as in what one's self may do. There is a terrible cumulative force in this kind of thing that may sweep away the strongest before he is aware. I doubt if you can honestly assert to yourself that your feeling is as cool and calm as it should be in a case of mere friendship, or, indeed, as it was two months ago."

That shot went home; the accused made no answer, but his face changed a little.

"Well, I must leave you now; it is just six o'clock, and I must go up to the church. I shall say no more. You must, of course, decide on your own course of action; only remember that Dendron's eyes are open. Things cannot be quite as they have been hitherto. You may save her from much unpleasantness if you are prompt."

He strode away; then stopped short and came back.

"I cannot go without thanking you for the way in which you have taken this—for the patience with which you have heard me."

Alick gave a queer sort of smile. "Well, I tried to keep my temper," he said; "I expect it was as hard for you to speak as for me to listen. Thanks."

Left alone, he clambered down a little way to a narrow ledge shut out from all but sea and sky, and sitting down on the short turf had it out with his conscience. For he was a man with a conscience, and perhaps a little over-confident in his own rectitude. Right and wrong meant to him something more definite than expediency or what made for the ultimate advantage of humanity. He was not of the stamp to tamper recklessly with a woman's reputation; he had no ambition to pose as the hero of a French novel; still less to figure in the divorce court. Confronted with the possible consequences of his summer's fooling, he felt much as if he had been awakened by a cold douche. His anger had evaporated; he honoured Septimus Jaques for speaking out as he had done. There was no more drifting possible now; the whole position stood out uncompromisingly before him in black and white, and he knew that one way or another his choice must be made.

From above his head the church bell swung out; just a few strokes, dying away into the absolute stillness. All the gorgeous colouring of the October afternoon—the emerald and violet of the sea, the rosy light in the sky, were fading into a cold grey. Even so the charm and glamour of the last few months was melting as he looked back at it. He was trying to do as Septimus had suggested; to look at his own conduct as though it had been another man's, and the result brought him to some unwelcome conclusions. A recollection came across him of his own words to her, spoken not so very long ago. It is so fatally easy to drift down the current, one forgets what it will cost to get back. And was the current already too strong for stemming? He tried to count what the cost would be of changing his manner, keeping away from Pencoet, risking chance encounters with Letty, and meeting her questioning reproachful eyes, and he knew very well he could not do it. He saw now what going too far meant. True, she had repulsed him that afternoon; but that counted for very little; next time, most likely, it would be different. He did not reckon much on a strength on her side that was lacking on his own. Then how utterly detestable it would be to feel that his altered behaviour was being watched and commented on. Even Septimus's approval would be like a blister. No, the only wise and indeed possible course was to cut the knot by going away and at once.

But there was another side. Reason might decide one way, but feeling must have her say too. All the charm, the intoxicating sweetness that had carried him off his feet that very day, swept over him again, and with it the passionate pity that was so large an ingredient in his feeling for Letty; it made it for the moment look almost right for him to stay. Mr. Jaques had said that her husband was awake to the local gossip that had coupled their names, and how might he not visit it upon her? It seemed mean to go off and leave her to face it alone, though, of course, a moment's reflection reminded him that it would in truth be the best chance of sparing her unpleasantness. He wanted terribly to see her just once, and explain why he thought he ought to go; it seemed brutal to go without a word. "But if I do," he said to himself, "it will be all up with me."

He sat there till the grey dusk had turned to the purple dark, forgetful of the three-mile walk to Hennacombe, forgetful of the rigorously punctual meal-times at the Rectory, and of all things save the trouble he was in.

When at length he got back, high tea was over, and Mr. Treby had already gone back to his study; a covered dish was reposing in the fender, and Rachel had turned back the corner of the tablecloth to make room for her inkstand and a whole phalanx of little account-books. She looked up at his entrance with a clouded brow.

"Really, Alick, I think you might remember how particular papa is about every one being in to meals. I have had to listen the whole of tea to a Jeremiad about your unpunctuality. I suppose you have had dinner, but I kept the chops warm as well as I could, in case you had not."

"No, I have not had anything. I have been wandering about with my gun, and forgot the time. It does not signify, thanks, I am not in the least hungry."

He sank wearily down in an armchair, stretching out his legs as though they were stiff.

"Nonsense!" she cried, lifting up the dish and ringing the bell. "I was going to say I would make some fresh tea, but you had much better have some hot whisky and water. I can't think what you can have been about to get so chilled and blue. Really you are too foolish; just as you are getting better, to go tiring yourself out for the sake of half a dozen rabbits. I have no patience with you."

While she scolded him, she was bringing a little table to his elbow, and attending to all his wants with a manner oddly compounded of indignation and a very real concern. By-and-by, when he was beginning to eat and drink and get somewhat thawed, she said—

"Did you give cook the rabbits? They will make a nice curry for to-morrow; papa was saying at dinner he had got quite sick of mutton."

He laughed guiltily. "My dear, I am very sorry; there are no rabbits. I had no luck this afternoon; the little wretches are as wild as chamois."

She looked straight into his eyes.

"You have been to Pencoet," she said.

"Excuse me, I have not."

There was a minute's silence, and the clock ticked in a loud, obtrusive way. Then Rachel rose and stood by the fire.

"I must speak," she said. "I know it seems very strange for me to mention such a thing to you; but there is no one else who will take the trouble to, and I will. If you do not pull up, you will get into a horrible scrape there. Do you know that the way you are going on is in everybody's mouth?"

There was no answer. He went on cutting bread as if he had not heard her, but his hand shook a little.

"I can't help it, if you are angry with me for speaking," she went on. "I can't bear to see it, it makes me miserable. I know she is a great deal more to blame than you are. I could make excuses for her if she were a young ignorant girl, but she is a woman of the world, and knows perfectly well what she is about."

He rose to his feet. "Hush," he said in a peremptory tone. "I forbid you to say one word about her."

He left the room, and the door slammed behind him.

She returned to her work, but her mind was no longer in it, and she found herself calculating twenty pence to a shilling, and twelve shillings to a pound, in defiance of all laws of arithmetic. She wondered if she had been to blame for speaking. Would it, after all, do more harm than good? She heard him moving about overhead, and wondered since he was so tired he did not rest. About half-past nine he came down again. Was he going to be very angry?

"Rachel," he said, in a dry, cold voice, "I have altered all my plans, and decided on going up to town to-morrow. I want to consult Sir Theophilus Seagrim again. If he reports me fit for duty, I shall probably be sent out to China again to rejoin my ship for the year or two she will still be there. If not, I think of trying Wiesbaden for a month or so. An old shipmate of mine is there, and it might set me up. In any case, I shall not be down here again for a long while. I meant to have told you after tea. I have been with my father in the study, and explained it all to him, and he says I can take the trap to drive in to Bridesworth to-morrow so as to catch an earlier train than I could by the Westcreek coach. So I shall probably be off before you are up, and I'll say good-bye to you now. I am not coming in to prayers; I have too much to do."

"Going? So suddenly! Why, Alick!"

He smiled grimly. I thought you would be relieved. I am afraid you have had rather too much of me this time."

Rachel looked startled.

"Is it—is it because of what I said?"

"No. I had decided on it before. You know I never talk of my plans till they are made."

She was perplexed and dissatisfied. "Has anything happened?" she asked.

"No. What should happen? If your mind is still running on what you spoke to me about just now, please put that entirely out of your head. I should be glad if you could promise never to allude to it again, either to me or to any one else. And remember, if there has been imprudence, she is in no way to blame."

"I will certainly promise. Oh, my dear, this is so sudden; it takes my breath away. Can't you wait just a day or two? I don't believe you are fit for that long journey yet."

"Oh, I shall do very well. My mind is made up. Now kiss me, Rachel, and wish me good-speed."

She put her arms round his neck as he stooped his tall head to hers.

"Oh, my dear boy, it breaks my heart to have you go like this. If I have been unjust to you, forgive me."

"All right, dear. I don't bear any malice." He returned her kiss gravely, and was gone.

CHAPTER X.

THE October mornings were getting chilly, and Letty had ordered a fire to be lighted in the panelled parlour. Only two days ago she had been having tea out upon the rocks, but that thunderstorm on Tuesday had completely broken up St. Luke's little summer, and the day was cold and rainy. She was easily affected by weather, and her spirits were down to zero. She had finished all her little housekeeping duties and arranged fresh chrysanthemums in the big china bowls, and it really seemed as if there would be nothing else to do before bedtime, and it was now only eleven o'clock. She drew an armchair in front of the fire and put up her feet on the fender as though it had been December.

She had a book in her lap, but she was not reading. She was sick of her Clarendon, sick of her "Seventeenth-century Love-letters," sick even of her Paul Bourget; or at least, if not quite that, certain suggestive passages in him sent her mind back to the very thing she was trying not to think of, and made her fling him down impatiently.

"What an idiot I was," she said to herself. "I wonder what he thought of me. I behaved like a schoolgirl. I wish he had not been so silly, but I ought to have been able to keep him in proper order. I must be more careful. I wonder he has not been here yet to see whether I have forgiven him. I suppose he will come by-and-by, and I must be very kind but firm, and ignore everything. I can't afford to lose him. Ah, how I missed him all yesterday. I suppose I really have been a trifle imprudent, and gone rather too far; but I shouldn't have done it if everybody hadn't winked and blinked and looked as if they thought my behaviour very shocking. Why, Rachel has not been near me for nearly a month, and I verily believe it is to mark her disapproval. From a child, I always would do whatever people told me I ought not—especially people who had no earthly business to interfere. As to Oliver, he does not care a pin what I do, or how I amuse myself; if he did—— Ah well, I suppose if I went off with any one, he would calmly say to the cook 'I don't expect your mistress back; I think you had better take the housekeeping;' and everything would go on just as usual. And yet I wish he would not keep watching me so; it makes me nervous. He never used to do it. I wonder if he has got anything in his head. If he has, I wish he would say so, and

I could assure him there is nothing in it, nothing; only one must amuse one's self."

She rose and tossed Paul Bourget away, and going to the piano, ran over some chords in a listless way, still standing; then she let herself sink on the music-stool and began to sing in her small but plaintive voice some lines she had met with in one of Mallock's books. He was a very favourite writer of hers; he just suited her idiosyncrasy; his intellectuality and his sensuousness; his intensely modern spirit and his exquisite appreciation of the past, appealed to her and expressed her to herself. She once said of his verses, in answer to a critic, "They may not be poetry of a very high order, but they suit me; they always make me feel as if I had written them myself. The lines she was singing now, and which she had set to music for herself, in her own incorrect but effective fashion, were these—

> " Yesterday a cloudless sky was glowing,
> All the flowers were flowering yesterday;
> And to-day a bitter east is blowing,
> Flowerless all the flowers, the skies are grey.
> Yesterday there breathed a life beside me— "

She broke off abruptly at this point. "No, I am not in the mood for singing," she said.

She strolled to the window, and stood a minute looking out.

"I wish Alick would come. I don't care for him one little bit, but I want him."

There was the sound of a horse coming down the lane; a heavy jog-trot.

"Only the postman. I wonder if he has got any home letters for me. I suppose the next will announce Sybil's engagement to Sir Edward Travers. How triumphant mother will be. I don't feel the least bit interested. Oh, only one?" as Susy Cann entered with one small missive on a salver.

She waited till the servant had retired, and then went back to her seat by the fire to open it. It was in Alick Studland's well-known firm, clear writing; it was very thin, and had a Bridesworth postmark. She looked perplexed as she broke the seal.

"My dear Mrs. Dendron,

"By the time this reaches you, I shall be in town, and I do not know what you will think of my rudeness in never calling to wish you good-bye. I can only plead in excuse that it was a sudden thing, and I am starting this morning early. I shall probably not be in Kerranstow again before I go out to China.

"With most grateful thanks for all your kindness and hospitality.—Yours very sincerely."

Letty dropped it on her lap. "Well!" she said. Then she picked it up again and turned it over, examining back and front, and even looking in the envelope to see if there might not be a bit more; but no, that was all, except that after the first paragraph there were two words scratched through with the pen. After much examination she managed to decipher "Will you—" Evidently the beginning of a sentence he had thought better of; but by itself conveying no meaning.

She sat staring into the fire for a long while. "This is Oliver's doing," she thought to herself, and her heart was hot with anger. What right had he to conclude that there was harm or danger in the friendship she had permitted herself? If he thought so, he should have taxed her with it, and given her the chance to explain. No less angry was she with Studland himself. It was for her to put an end to the intimacy if she thought proper; for him to draw back was an affront.

Presently the door into the dining-hall opened, and her husband came through, with his soft, slow step.

"Have you had letters from home, Letty?" he asked.

"No, why? You are not generally much interested about my people."

"It was only that it occurred to me that, now the dull autumn weather is coming on, you might be the better for a little change and variety; I thought, perhaps, if you went to your mother's for a while?"

She felt almost inclined to answer, "You need not concern yourself; he is gone;" but checked the reckless impulse, and said—

"My dear Oliver, what an absurd idea. You know mother is never at home at this time of year. They are staying at Travers Court."

"Oh, I did not know. Well, if they should be thinking of going abroad later, as I know they sometimes do in the winter, and you should like to join them, do not hesitate on the score of expense. I could manage it, and I should be very glad if you could."

"You seem very anxious to get rid of me," said Letty, looking straight at him.

He looked down at his boots in an embarrassed way.

"Pray do not put it in that way," he said, with that formal politeness that always irritated her more than anything. "I assure you it is only that I am aware that this country life is solitary and dull for you; and I should be pleased if you could make any agreeable changes."

"Thanks. But, at any rate, we have not been dull this summer; I consider Kerranstow has been quite gay with so many visitors. By the way, did you know that Mr. Studland was leaving so soon?"

"Studland? No; when is he going?" His countenance changed a little.

"He is gone already. I have just had a note of apology instead of a P.P.C. call. You would like to see it, perhaps; I had it here just now. Ah! there it is." She tossed it over to him, and added, "There is not a word to you, which I call very uncivil."

Oliver read it through in dead silence, laid it down on the mantelpiece, and left the room.

"Now," said Letty, "had he anything to do with it, or had he not? What a thing it is to have to do with a sphinx!"

Kerranstow was aggrieved. It had been waiting

open-mouthed for a *dénouement*, and when none came, it felt itself defrauded of a legitimate entertainment. That Studland should go, and so abruptly, was indeed matter for comment; but when his disappearance seemed to leave Pencoet totally unaffected, there was a flatness and tameness about the whole thing that, to the least uncharitable, savoured of disappointment. Speculation, which at first was very lively, soon died out, like a fire of dead leaves, for want of something to feed on, and the whole matter was soon put by and forgotten, like last year's snow.

But Mrs. Twisselton, at least, was equal to elaborating a version that seemed to meet all the requirements of the case. She wrote out to Wimmelhahn to the following effect—

"I know you are interested in all that goes on here, and though you pretended not to see what was passing under your nose even when I pointed it out to you—you absurd, innocent little puss—you must be dying to know how it all ended. Things got to such a pass that I felt it my duty to open Mr. Dendron's eyes; and I am not one who ever shrinks from a duty, however painful. He acted upon my hint immediately. Of course I cannot tell you exactly what passed; but I have reason to think he threatened Mr. Studland with legal proceedings unless he left the place at once. He was gone the next morning, and when I heard it, I thought nothing else than that she had gone too; but there she is, and very much subdued, I can tell you. I feel very thankful that I should have been the humble instrument, under Providence, of putting a stop to a scandal which, I can assure you, quite preyed upon my spirits. She has never liked me; but, of course, she has no suspicion that it was I who roused her husband to a sense of his duty.

"I could have made some excuse for Mr. Studland's absurd infatuation if she had been a handsome woman ; but what he could see in a little wisp of a creature like that, with yellow eyes, like a sandy kitten, passes my comprehension."

And then the writer passed on to other matters ; the shape of the winter bonnets as seen in the shop-windows at Bridesworth, and speculations as to why Denis Kay had packed up his traps and given notice to give up his studio at Peninah Sutton's for good.

So Kerranstow ceased from watching Pencoet, and returned to its ploughing and sowing, its fiddling and carving, as heretofore; but now that the little group who had made merry all the summer through were scattered, it was lonely for the few that remained behind, and the gaps were felt for many a long month.

CHAPTER XI.

STEFAN NICOLAI was considered by far the best master in Wimmelhahn, and to be taught by him at all was something of a distinction. If a new pupil at the Conservatoire were tried and found wanting, she was handed over without scruple to an underling, however able or willing she might be to pay the highest fees. Jenifer was fully alive to the honour done her when she found herself assigned to Herr Nicolai's tuition; but it was an honour that involved a degree of application she had never been used to, in order to live up to it.

The morning after she had received her cousin's letter of Kerranstow gossip she failed conspicuously to come up to her master's requirements. It was the custom there for two girls to take their violin lesson together; they studied the same piece, and while one played it, the other was supposed to listen to the master's corrections, and carry them out when her turn to play the same passage came. Sometimes they played together, but not often.

On this occasion, Jenifer's thoughts were at Kerranstow, and Fraulein Waldstein's blunders, and Herr Nicolai's comments, alike fell on inattentive ears. Presently it was her turn to play; the piece before her was a difficult study in six flats; a test of mechanical dexterity and quickness in reading rather than an utterance of emotion, and Jenifer was not in the mood to give her mind to anything that did not appeal to her feelings. She got as far as an intricate succession of double notes, and then came to grief. She missed a note, harked back, lost the time, and just as she thought she was going to recover herself, Nicolai's bow rapped sharply on the desk to stop her, and she pulled up in confusion.

"I think I requested you last week, mein Fraulein, to practise those bars repeatedly," said the master with severity.

"But I have; I have gone over them over and over again—twenty times, I should think."

"Then have the goodness to go over them two hundred and twenty times at your next practice."

"It is a horrid bit; I cannot manage it; I shall never do it," said Jenifer, rebelliously.

Nicolai shrugged his shoulders.

"You would probably prefer something easier," he said. "Very well, it is all the same to me. I will arrange your transference to another class. I should recommend Engelhardt. You could not have a better man; he is excellent—for amateurs."

Jenifer flashed round at that. "I am not an amateur," she exclaimed.

"Are you not? That remains to be proved."

She thought him unjust. She had been working harder than she had ever done in her life before, and it was all so new to her, the effort and strain of constant application was double what it would be to those who had grown accustomed to it; but she would not make excuses. She felt as if she could have cried, but she held her little head high, and said quietly—

"Very well, mein Herr, you will of course arrange it as you please. Am I to understand that I continue this lesson or not?"

"Yes of course; you can go on to the next *étude*. Stay——" He looked at her doubtfully. "Suppose you try over that passage once more."

She paused. "I am not quite sure that I understand it," she said; "the time is very catchy, and I cannot hear it in my mind's ear."

He took the violin from her, and laying it on his shoulder, swept through the passage in question, with his inimitable turn of wrist, as though it were a mere cadenza, and then handed back the instrument with a bow and a quizzical look.

"What a shame," inwardly commented Gisela Waldstein, as she watched her fellow-pupil with anxiety. "That will only make it ten times more difficult for her. One could hardly even hear it at that pace. Nicolai has no mercy."

But Jenifer took her fiddle back, and leaning her

head down as though she were still listening, followed his rendering—not indeed with absolute correctness, but with exactly the same phrasing, the same sweep, gathering together the notes into just the rush of meaning he had given them.

He looked at her with a new expression.

"Ah, that is coming," he said. "Go on working it up on those lines. Time is up. Good-morning, ladies."

He brought his heels together, and made a low bow as he left the classroom.

"What a brute Nicolai was to you this morning, Miss Lyon," said Gisela, as they put up their fiddles and collected their music. "I am sure I should have cried. I can't bear anybody to speak to me like that; it upsets me so. Do you know, if I were you, I should not be at all sorry to be sent to Engelhardt. He is so charming and so very good-looking, and although of course he isn't such a genius as Nicolai, I am not at all sure he does not teach quite as well. He is infinitely kinder, and he does not make one grind so. Of course Nicolai is the fashion; it is the thing here to be taught by him, but Engelhardt is really just as good a master."

"Perhaps so," said Jenifer. "I often think the second rank of performers make the best teachers; I suppose they can enter into the difficulties of learning more. All the same, I don't relish being sent down. And, after all, though I was stupid this afternoon, I don't want an easy-going master."

"Well, I dare say if you eat humble-pie, Nicolai will take you back, but I should not, if I were you; you will be much happier with Engelhardt."

"Ah, you think I am not equal to this class?"

"No, no," said Gisela, who was a kind-hearted girl; I believe you are really much cleverer than I am; but, you see, I have been regularly trained ever since I was five, and you are not used to the grind. Nicolai is such a Jew. A Hungarian Jew is a terrible compound, when it comes to music."

At the corner of the street, Jenifer parted with her companion. It was not quite teatime, and she thought she would turn down to the Thiergarten for a little quiet. She had been a good deal fretted and ruffled, and she was so used to solitude that she felt she needed to be by herself to face her difficulties. Solitude such as she was accustomed to on the Kerranstow cliffs was indeed not attainable anywhere in Wimmelhahn, except on such a long country walk as she was not allowed to take alone; but at the farther end of the Thiergarten were long green alleys, almost deserted in the late autumn afternoons, and the occasional appearance of a broad-faced German student with his arm round the waist of his "Schatz" in no way disturbed her meditations.

She had been here long enough now to have reached that point of discouragement which most people find sooner or later lying in wait for them, on a new venture far from home and from all accustomed surroundings. She was home-sick, of course; that goes without saying. Cornish born and bred, in this inland, wooded spot she hungered for the bare granite cliffs and the wide sea with a hunger that was like a physical need. She was struggling through the drudgery of her work with weakened powers, and for the moment the success, the beauty, the charm of her playing seemed all overlaid and lost sight of. She felt snubbed and humiliated by Nicolai's severity, so cruelly contrasted in her memory with the vicar's encouraging criticisms and Yeo's admiring pride in her performance. In her disappointment, she felt almost inclined to act on Gisela's advice, to give up struggling, to allow herself to sink to the easy level of Engelhardt, and to renounce the vain dream of ever becoming a great violinist.

Little as she would admit it to herself, Louisa's letter had its part in her depression. It was nothing to her, of course; Alick Studland, and what he did had long ceased to have any concern for her, yet Louisa's reports and vulgar comments were like a rude touch on a scarce-healed wound. She tried not to think of it, but it added its quota to her restless discontent. Since she had come to Wimmelhahn she had felt as though she were asleep and dreaming. The life was so new, so different, she seemed completely sundered from her old self; but to-day she had suddenly found herself again, and realized that she had brought all her old thoughts and troubles with her, only they had been put to sleep for awhile.

She was fairly happy in her new surroundings. Frau Klieschmann, and her daughter were kind and friendly, and she had easily accommodated herself to their foreign ways. But their kindness was not of the sort that took from her her sense of being alone. They were not people she could turn to for advice or support. Wilhelmina wore a string of beads round her neck, tied with a bow of ribbon with long floating ends; she was "*schwärmerisch*," and gushed about the first tenor at the Opera; she made so many confidences about him to Jenifer that the latter in her simplicity concluded that they must be engaged or on the brink of becoming so, and was quite bewildered when one day at an open-air concert a friend, who was probably also in the secret of Mina's enthusiasm, brought him up to their table, and introduced him to both girls, and instead of greeting him as an old friend, Mina was so overwhelmed at the unexpected honour that she sank into abashed silence, and let him direct all his conversation to her companion. If she had been consulted on the subject of Jenifer's difficulties at the Conservatoire she would probably have considered, as Fraulein Waldstein did, that Engelhardt's blue eyes and blond moustache were worth a great deal more than Nicolai's genius, and that any girl might consider herself lucky in having to practise four hours instead of eight, and learn pretty things instead of those everlasting études and fugues.

But Jenifer could not so easily lay aside the

ambition which had animated her, and which had been strong enough to induce her home-loving nature to break all ties, and venture forth into the great unknown world. If her music was to be a mere ornamental appendage, she might as well not have come.

She turned down a narrow path between a thicket of alder and white poplar, and walked quickly as though bent on reaching some goal, though in truth she was only driven forward by her hurrying thoughts. It was very still; the leaves came dropping softly, spinning and fluttering like yellow moths before they reached the ground; but she took no heed of them.

Presently a sound broke the stillness; men's voices singing in parts, rising and falling in some Volkslied with a swinging refrain. A party of Burschen on their way home from work, stopping at some distant Trinkhalle, no doubt. Neither words nor tune had the slightest reference to the subject of her thoughts, yet in the odd way that often happens with very musically constituted people, the music seemed to rouse her to a clearness of vision she had not had before, and to quicken all her faculties.

She saw that she had come to one of those critical moments of choice that now and then present themselves, and which may mean the making or marring of a life. The choice between the two masters meant the choice of her career. Was it to be Engelhardt and an easy life with young-lady music—very much above the average, it is true—good enough to enable her to teach, when she went back to England; or was it to be Nicolai, and all her time and strength absorbed in work, and at the end—what? "Ah, if I only knew," she said to herself; "but if he will have me, I think I will risk it."

She had realized, what very few people find out till they are a good deal more than nineteen, that though there may be a fair amount of happiness in the world, there is not quite enough to go round, and that hers was to be one of the lots that come short. She knew that her heart's desire would never be hers; she had deliberately refused the marriage of esteem which had been offered her, and in which most women could have found a very satisfying kind of happiness, and now she saw that unless she was prepared to devote herself wholeheartedly to the pursuit in which she might hope to excel, she ran the risk of sinking into that too numerous class of low-spirited women who seem to have no life of their own, but are mere hangers-on to other people's.

When she reached this point she turned and walked steadily homewards, and arriving there, shut herself up in her practising-room resolved upon a literal two-hundred-and-twenty-times repetition of the offending passage which had been the cause of her morning's troubles.

Next Tuesday it so fell out that Fraulein Waldstein had a severe toothache, so Jenifer must betake herself to her lesson alone, and hardly knew whether she was to present herself at Herr Nicolai's classroom or not. She entered timidly.

"Do I take my lesson with you, mein Herr, or have you spoken to Herr Engelhardt about me?"

"Not yet; we will see."

She made Fraulein Waldstein's apologies, and began tuning her instrument, wondering the while whether she had better make any reference to her failure last week, and beg for mercy, or wait upon events. She chose the latter course, and following the usual routine, began her study in E flat minor. He listened in silence to her rendering of the vexed passage, only nodding his head slightly at the end with a curt, "*Das geht.*" Then he bade her play a romance by Ries, in which she was much more at home, and even condescended to play her accompaniment himself, a duty usually performed by the companion pupil.

When she had finished, he rose from the piano without a word, and taking up his violin, began absently to play some little random passages, and looking away from her, he said—

"I am afraid I was very rough on you last week, Miss Lyon."

She smiled up at him. The great Nicolai apologizing was a thing hardly to be believed.

"You were a little hard upon me, mein Herr. I am sorry I was so stupid; I had had letters from home, and I am afraid that made me inattentive."

"Ah, those letters! That is just where it is. I

wish I could taboo the postman. You would do very well if nobody wrote to you. While you are studying you ought to shut eyes, ears, and mind to everything outside music."

"If I only could!" sighed Jenifer.

"So! Do you mean that really? If I thought so—but I know just how it is with you young ladies. You come here because the fiddle, for its sins, has become the fashion——"

"I don't," put in Jenifer; "the fashion is nothing to me."

"Full of enthusiasm," he went on, without listening to her interruption, "and often with thrice the facility of lads of your age, and one fancies one has found a phœnix, and one spends one's heart's blood teaching you, and then come letters from home, or you pick up some young fellow at the Thiergarten concerts, and one finds the music was only assumed as an additional attraction, like the *toupée* or the paint. I have had enough of you. I have often said I will have no more girls. I will wash my hands of women pupils; I will teach only men."

He was striding up and down the room now, his mobile Semitic face alight with an odd mixture of anger and enthusiasm. He came to a halt in front of Jenifer, and she answered—

"Is it any use, mein Herr, to assure you that the violin shall have my whole devotion?"

"H'm. You mean it seriously at the time, I know; so do they all. I wonder if you have counted the cost?"

"I think I have. I want to do my utmost. It is the only thing I care for, or am ever likely to care for."

He looked at her oddly. "You are almost a child," he said. "I wonder if you understand what you are talking about?"

She ignored that, and went on—

"I know I must seem very backward beside Fräulein Waldstein, but remember how long she has been at work; and though I used to fancy I was working at it, till I came here I don't think I knew what work meant."

"Oh, I know. She comes of professional people, and has been trained from her babyhood; it isn't fair to compare you. But you have something that she has not, and it is precisely that that makes you so perplexing and disappointing to teach, so that I get all out of patience with you."

"I am sorry," said Jenifer, penitently.

He took another turn, and then went on—

"There are things that come to her like her A B C that you, for no earthly reason that I can comprehend, stumble and baulk at; and then, again, there are things that I could never make her understand till Doomsday that you catch at once, without a word of explanation. The inner meaning of a thing you always seem to know without my telling. You remember that thing of Schumann's that I made her give up? You played it as though Schumann himself had showed you how. But you are so terribly uncertain. That is what you must overcome. The brain can conceive, if only the hand will do."

She looked up bewildered. The tone in which the words were spoken made them sound like a reproach.

"I don't know what it is——" she began, and stopped, puzzled at his expression.

"Don't you? Don't you, indeed?" He was leaning on the desk, and he bent forward and stretched out his bow till the point of it just touched her cheek. "Why, that is genius," he said.

She bent her head. "It almost frightens me," she murmured.

"I knew you would take it like that, or I should hardly have told you. If I thought you would presume upon it to work less you should never have heard it from me. One of your great writers—Carlyle or Arnold, or I forget who—has said that genius is a sublime capacity for taking trouble. Like most aphorisms, it is profoundly untrue; it is nothing of the sort; but it is the one thing that makes it supremely worth while to take trouble."

She looked up as he paused.

"But if you really think this of me, mein Herr, you will help me? You will not send me to Herr Engelhardt?"

"Pshaw! Of course not; Engelhardt shall not have you. I never meant it really; it was a bit of temper because just as I thought you were getting on you disappointed and provoked me. But I was rather afraid you meant to take me at my word. Himmel! how late it is! Do you know how much time we have wasted talking? I must fly."

He laid his fiddle in its case, and then instead of the customary stiff bow in the doorway, he approached Jenifer, and held out his hand.

"You will give me a real English shake-hands, nicht wahr?"

"How late you are, my dear!" said Frau Klieschmann, when Jenifer came in. "The coffee is quite cold. I will have in the kettle, and make you a nice cup of tea for a treat. I suppose you walked round with Gisela Waldstein?"

"No," said Jenifer, "Gisela has the toothache, poor girl, and could not go, so I had my lesson alone, and it was rather a long one."

"Alone!" cried Mina. "Oh, I say! Didn't you wish it had been Engelhardt?"

Jenifer laughed. "No, why should I?"

"Well, you look as if something very exciting had just happened to you, does not she, mamma? Did you, oh, did you meet Blumenfeld?"

Jenifer shook her head, and professed herself unable to see why a chance encounter with the tenor should record itself on any one's countenance.

"Then," said the persistent questioner, "I am sure Nicolai must have made you an offer; you look as if you were walking on air."

"Herr Nicolai made me nothing more exciting

than an apology for scolding me unmercifully last week."

"An apology! Nicolai! Jenifer, you must be dreaming."

"Well, he followed it up with a lecture, and a very long study in double notes which I am going to work at directly after tea," said Jenifer, soberly. "Mina, you are too absurd."

"I can only say," said the irrepressible, handing her her cup, "if that is the effect of a lecture, I wish Madame Schmidt would give me one every week at my singing-lesson."

Walking on air truly she felt, and her heart was still throbbing, and her cheeks glowing when half an hour later she shut herself up in her little practising den.

"That is genius." Not all the encomiums, and encouragements she had ever received had come near that. And Nicolai had said it; he who was so harsh, so exacting, so slow to admit progress. Supremely worth while, indeed, to toil with such a goal before her. She had murmured sometimes for need of happiness, and now a key was put into her hand which would unlock for her the door into a joy more intense than happiness, and keener than pain. The assurance, as Nicolai had foreseen, gave her faith. The sense of her own insufficiency had hitherto baulked her, and marred the perfect solace she would have found in her music: she wanted self-confidence; but with his word to back her, she would have it now. He could trust her, and better than that, she would trust herself.

She would never tell anybody what he had said to her; that should be a secret between him and her alone. She laid it away in her memory beside another remembrance of a voice she once used to love, saying — "I like your playing, Jenifer; it is like singing."

BOOK III.

> "*Duchess.* What do you think of marriage?
> *Antonio.* I take it as those that deny purgatory;
> It locally contains or heaven or hell;
> There's no third place in't."
>   WEBSTER'S *Duchess of Malfy.*

CHAPTER I.

MORE than a year has gone by, bringing but little in the way of change to Pencoet. In fact, we find Letty Dendron sitting in precisely the same armchair, in almost the same attitude in which we left her reading her brief farewell epistle from Alick Studland. The only perceptible difference is that, since it is evening, she is wearing an Empire tea-gown of a peculiar shade of reddish heliotrope, very becoming to her fair skin. She does not look a day older; women of her type usually wear well, and there is not much fatigue or worry about her present lotus-eating existence. Her fair, fluffy curls shine like a child's, and there are as yet no lines under her eyes; just a shade more discontent, that is all.

This was the second winter since Studland went away, and to her they had certainly been dull ones. There were no village concerts and no local dances—as, indeed, how should there be, for where were partners to come from? Denis Kay, too, seemed to have snapped his connection with Kerranstow, and nothing had been heard of him for a long time, even by his faithful Peninah. John Yeo and the brothers Polsue had indeed played their trios as of old, but it was Jenifer who had supplied the connecting link with the "quality," and in her absence Letty ceased to take any interest in their performances. Septimus Jaques buried himself in his books, and Rachel Treby tried to smother her dulness under a multitude of guilds, mothers' unions, and choir teas.

At present there was no prospect for Letty of escape from the surroundings she had wearied of; Oliver's affairs were still far from having recovered; he declared another year's economy absolutely necessary, and as she agreed she would rather endure it here than try to make an appearance on insufficient means, they had taken on the old house for a year more.

The maid entered with the coffee, and Letty looked round surprised. Latterly Oliver had taken to following her into the drawing-room soon after she left the table, where he would sit on the opposite side of the fire with the paper in his hand, reading out bits and making occasional comments on them with a laudable, but too evidently conscientious desire to entertain her. To-night, though it was past nine o'clock, he had not appeared.

"You had better take the coffee into the

study, Fanny," she said, as she poured cream into her own cup; "your master never stays long in the dining-room. I expect he had letters to write."

She put her cup on the little table beside her, and buried herself again in the *Fortnightly*, which she had been reading. She hardly observed that the servant passed through the room again, still carrying the tray, as if in search of her master; for the dining-hall was reached by a door from the panelled parlour.

In another minute she was roused from her book. Fanny was standing in the doorway, looking startled.

"Please, ma'am, would you come here? I am afraid master is ill; I cannot make him hear."

Letty put down her book and went to the door. The lamp on the sideboard had been carried out, and the four candles on the table with their red shades gave but a feeble and uncertain light in the large, dark, panelled room. Oliver's back was towards her; he seemed to be leaning forwards over the table. She went nearer to him, exclaiming—

"Why, Oliver, have you fallen asleep? Any one who did not know you would think you had been indulging too freely."

He was such an abstemious man that the little jest was harmless enough. She bent over him and laid a hand on his shoulder.

"Wake up. Here is the coffee."

Then her voice changed.

"Bring the light nearer, quick! Take off the shade. He is in a fit."

But when the light shone upon his face she drew back with a sudden, sharp cry, while Fanny burst out—

"Oh, he's dead, he's dead! Whatever shall us do!"

In a moment, the cook, who heard a scream, came running in through the buttery hatch at the far end, and added her quota to Fanny's wailing; then broke off to put her strong arms round her mistress's waist, begging her not to take on. But it was Letty who first recovered her presence of mind.

"Never mind me, cook. Run quick to the cottage and tell Jacob to saddle the mare and ride in to Widcombe for Dr. Shapcot, and tell Bobby to run as fast as ever he can to the Vicarage, and beg Mr. Jaques to come to me. Stop, let Fanny go, and you stay with me. You are older; you have seen more of illness. Is there nothing we can do? Oh, do let us try something."

They pushed back his chair from the table, preparatory to trying to move him on to a sofa, but the way the nerveless arms dropped at his side and his head sunk forwards on his breast showed that it was too late for any remedies. It was horrible to stand there watching him in silent helplessness, and at length Letty suffered herself to be drawn unresisting into the next room, and let the servant close the door, shutting in the awful mystery. Yet she kept starting from her seat every moment, feeling as if it were wicked to leave him there alone. She felt dazed, and it might almost have seemed like some horrid dream, but for the unnatural presence of cook in the drawing-room, sitting very forward on the edge of the sofa with her apron to her eyes, giving vent to occasional prolonged snuffles. Now and then she caught herself saying in her own mind, "If only Oliver were here he would tell me what to do."

Wonderfully soon, almost before she had begun to allow herself to expect it, there was a sound of footsteps crunching outside, and the opening of the hall door. She ran out, but paused as she heard the vicar's solemn tones, saluting the house, as he crossed the threshold. Then, hardly pausing to shake the snow from his shoulders where it lay in a fine powder, he came towards her holding out both hands, his face full of pity.

"Is it as bad as little Bob tells me? Is all over?"

She gripped his hands and held them like a vice as she drew him into the dim, ghostly hall where the dead man still sat beside the uncleared table.

There was no need to repeat the question. The vicar closed the eyes and crossed the helpless hands, while Letty whispered that they had not dared to move him when they saw that it was no use; then, motioning her to kneel beside him, he put up a prayer for the departed soul. Nothing could so have brought home to Letty the reality of what had happened to her, and she shivered as he rose from his knees and led her into the other room.

She crossed to the fire, and, mutely refusing the chair he pushed forwards, knelt on the fender-stool, holding out her chilled hands to the blaze.

He looked at her with a strange mixture of pity and perplexity. His heart was strongly moved on behalf of the dead man whose trouble he had perhaps understood better than any one else; yet Letty, in her forlorn dismay, appealed to his compassion. She looked so like a child with her white cheeks and dark hollows under her eyes, with her curls all ruffled and pushed back from her forehead, as she crouched on the low stool, her quaint limp draperies falling about her slim figure. He hardly knew what to say; if she had wept and lamented he could have consoled; as it was, his first remark was sufficiently commonplace.

"You are cold, and the fire has got down; let me make it up for you. It is a bitter night, and snowing; I am afraid it may be some hours before Shapcot can get here. You mean to stay up for him? You would like me to remain with you till he comes?"

"Oh, please, if you don't mind."

She gave a shuddering glance at the closed door at the far end of the room.

There was silence again. The flame flickered up round the wood that had just been put on and crackled noisily. Septimus walked to the window, and drawing aside the heavy curtain, peered out into the night.

"The ground is getting quite white," he said, "and it lies thick upon the window-ledges."

She made no answer; she was not listening. He came back and seated himself beside her.

"Would it distress you to speak of what has happened?" he began. "Had you any idea that Mr. Dendron was out of health?"

She answered his thought rather than his words.

"Oh," she said, "how heartless and unfeeling you must think me because I do not cry; but I can't cry. I think I am too frightened, and, besides, I don't believe it. I don't believe it," she repeated. "Why, I keep thinking how strange Oliver will think it when I tell him in the morning."

"You ought to have some one with you," said Mr. Jaques, with apparent irrelevance. "Wouldn't you like to send for some one?—your mother? It is too late to telegraph to-night, but we could send a telegram to her the first thing in the morning. Dr. Shapcot could take one in, and send it off from Widcombe. That would save time."

"Oh, I don't think mother could possibly come to me. She is with my sister, Lady Travers, and they can't spare her till after the baby is born; but perhaps she would send me Violet. One can't say all that in a telegram. I had better write; only I am so mazed, I don't know what to say."

"I will write for you."

He went to the writing-table, and for some time Letty listened to the scratching of his pen; then she rose softly and began to walk down the room towards the dining-hall. In a moment Mr. Jaques was beside her and took her hand.

"Where are you going?" he asked.

She drew her hand away impatiently.

"I am only going in there to see if he is there still—if he has moved."

"You must not go in there any more to-night. I think you had better go upstairs to bed, and keep one of the servants with you. This vigil is bad for you. I will stay and see Shapcot when he comes."

"No, no, let me stay." Her voice was piteous.

He made her sit in the armchair, and drew round the great leather screen. Sitting so she could not see the door into the other room. Presently she roused herself.

"I ought to have offered you something after your cold walk and staying up so late. How inhospitable of me! What will you have?" Her hand was on the bell.

"Never mind me. I had dined before your message came. Still, I would not say no to a cup of hot tea if you will have some too."

That brought a smile to her face—a smile that was quenched the next instant in a sense of its wickedness—for the vicar's partiality for tea was a standing joke; but she rang and gave the order, feeling that any sort of occupation would be a relief. But when it was brought in by Fanny, ostentatiously hysterical, she leaned back and hid her eyes, ashamed of her own dry-eyed apathy. She suffered him to usurp the woman's office of tea-maker, but when he placed a cup on a little stand by her side, she drank it gratefully, and began to feel that the dumb chill in which she had been wrapped was giving way a little.

Then, seeing the good effect of his suggestion, he began his queries anew.

"Had he been complaining of illness lately? Had you any reason to be afraid of any sudden attack?"

"No," said Letty, in a more natural voice; "but, you know, he never did complain. If he had been really ill, I don't suppose he would have let me know it. I have certainly thought him looking out of health the last few weeks. There was a sort of white look about him at times, and then little things tried him so; but I never dreamt of there being anything serious the matter."

"Were you with him when he was taken ill?"

"No, he was quite alone. I never noticed anything amiss at dinner. He did not eat much, it is true, but he has grown very faddy about his food lately, so I did not take any notice. And now I come to think of it, he was more silent than usual; but then, you know, he never is talkative at any time."

She had not yet brought herself to use the past tense in speaking of him.

"Usually," she went on, "he has come into the drawing-room to me before the coffee came in, instead of spending his evenings in his own study, as he used to do. I suppose he thought I was dull alone."

A little quiver came into her voice as she recalled with remorse how bored she had often been with those scraps of stale news out of the *St. James's*, and how she used to wish she were at liberty to go on undisturbed with her own book.

"And to-night he did not come?" put in Mr. Jaques. "Did you go and look for him?"

"No, not till Fanny came in. I never thought anything but that he had something to read or had fallen asleep; but she was frightened when she could not get him to move or speak, and called me. And when I went in, he sat there in his chair by the table, just where I had left him only an hour before, leaning forward a little. Oh, it is not possible!"—she started up again—"he can't be dead!"

"My poor child, there isn't any doubt about it; but if it will make you any easier I will take you in to look upon him just once more."

There was an indescribable awfulness about the sight. Mr. Jaques had judged it right to leave the body as it was found until the doctor's arrival, with the exception of closing the eyes and placing the hanging hands in a more reverent posture; but it was ten times more ghastly to see the dead man sitting there in his correct evening dress than it would have been to see him lying straight in snowy shroud in a room darkened and decently prepared. On the table stood Letty's dainty decorations of flowers and sweetmeats and rose-shaded candles, now almost burnt down to their sockets, and close to his hand was a plate with the *débris* of grapes and walnuts.

But about the great central fact there was not any doubt. No living man ever wore that air of awful stillness; no breathing lips could be set in that ineffably rigid and changeless smile.

Septimus stood looking at him till the tears gathered in his own eyes and brimmed over. He had stood by many a corpse, but never by one which touched him with a sharper pity. Such a lonely life, and such a lonely death. Even the new-made widow seemed to feel horror and dread rather than grief. He turned away from her. He would rather have shed those tears when she was not by to see his weakness, but he was a man of quick feeling, and the scene was so indescribably piteous. But Letty saw that he was moved, and in some subtle way it woke her dormant feelings. She threw up her hands with a gesture of despair.

"Oh," she cried, "and I stand here like a stone! If he could only hear me say I am sorry, I am sorry. I feel now as if I could throw myself at his feet and beg him to forgive me; but he seems so unutterably far away." Her voice was suddenly quenched in sobs.

Mr. Jaques did not speak till they were back in the other room; then he said—

"I wish he could hear you say that."

Letty wept on for some time; then she broke out again—

"I know I never made him as happy as I might have done. I was always meaning to try, but it is so difficult to change; and now that it is too late, it all comes home to me. I don't mean that we did not get on well together," she went on, looking up and speaking more steadily. "We never quarrelled, and he was always most kind and considerate, only we always seemed so far apart. It was a great deal my fault; I believe if I had tried in the first place, I could have made him care for me."

"Care for you!" said Septimus, and paused. "Now that he can never explain himself to you, I think it would not be a breach of confidence if I were to tell you what he once said to me, more than a year ago. 'God gave me my desire, and sent leanness withal into my soul.' You will best understand what he meant."

He was silent, and Letty's head went down again upon her knees. He let her cry on till she raised her head and said—

"Why does one never know these things till too late? I thought if I were indifferent, he was at least as indifferent. I never meant to take all and give nothing. My people wanted me to marry a man with means, and I supposed he wanted a wife who was in society and well-connected, and that sort of thing. But he never made love to me; it wasn't in him, I suppose, so how could I tell?"

"He was very reserved; but I think there was a great deal underlying that coldness of manner."

"I suppose there was. I never felt as if I knew him. I remember when we were engaged I thought him a quiet sort of man without much in him, and I recollect saying to one of my sisters, 'At any rate, I shall always have my own way.' I did have it, but not because I took it, but because he gave it me; and I thought he gave it me because he did not care. He was like granite."

The vicar remembered how Oliver once had said, "I thought I could have moulded her to my will; she was so young." How grievously mistaken they had been in each other!

"I never professed to be in love with him," Letty went on, with the natural rebound from self-accusation to self-justification. "I had had a great deal of trouble, and there are so many of us. Mamma was very anxious we should marry early. I thought at the time I was acting unselfishly, for it really was not fair to keep Sybil in the schoolroom any longer."

Letty's tears were dried now, and she was talking herself into self-complacency again. It was a difficult and delicate task for any pastor who felt his responsibilities as this man did. In one sense it was too late for any exhortations to be of any avail, and he wondered sadly whether he might not have done anything to heal the breach before death had let down the curtain; yet there had been no overt difference, and no outsider could have interfered. He spoke such words of counsel as he thought she needed, and when she had cried herself weary, he induced her to lie down upon the sofa, and drawing a book from his pocket, retired to a distant lamp and read while another hour wore itself away.

Wheels at last. Letty had fallen into a doze, so he stepped softly into the hall, drawing the door close after him. Dr. Shapcot entered, the front of his thick driving-coat caked with snow like a twelfth-cake, and his beard covered with icicles.

"I expected this," were his first words. "The only wonder to me is that it had not happened before."

"I am thankful to hear you say so, for then there need be no inquiry, I suppose?"

"Oh no, no. I can testify to valvular disease of the heart. It must have been a terrible shock to that poor young thing, though. He would not have her told."

"He was aware of his own danger, then?"

"Perfectly. He had known it a year or more. Well, we will go in."

"I suppose I had better see her," said the doctor, as they came out of the hall which they had entered by the lower end in order not to disturb Letty. Mr. Jaques led the way silently to the drawing-room. Exhausted by the fatigues and emotions of the night, she had slept so soundly that the tread of the two men in the adjoining room, softened as it was out of reverence for the dead, had not roused her. There she lay, her hand under her cheek like a baby's, the fur rug pushed aside showing the folds of her dainty dress flowing over the cushions. Resting from the fatigues of a ball, any one who had seen her might have said, but for her matted eyelashes and a slight stain of tears on her cheek. They stood side by side for a minute looking at her. Then the doctor spoke. He was one of Letty's most ardent admirers; but there was a sardonic look on his face as he said—

"There is no need of a composing draught here, I think. Let her maid get her to bed without rousing her more than she can help, and she will go off to sleep again like a child. Shall I drive you up to the Vicarage?"

"Strange," he said presently to his silent companion, as the dog-cart ploughed its way through the snow. "It is just these soft, sympathetic, tender sort of women who, when the pinch comes, seem to have no heart. One used to pity her for being tied to that stick — God forgive me for speaking so of the dead — but I doubt the saddle was on the wrong horse all the while."

CHAPTER II.

ONE afternoon Wilhelmina came bursting into Jenifer's practising room, waving a minute card.

"A visitor for you! Put away your fiddle, and tidy your hair, and come down quick."

But Jenifer only paused with suspended bow, and, without even looking at the card, said with some irritation—

"How could Gretchen be so stupid as to let anybody in; she knows I never see visitors in practising time."

"But he has come from England on purpose, and he wouldn't go away. 'Denis Kay,'" she read off the card. "Oh, do tell me whether he is the artist Muriel thinks such a lot of?"

"Mr. Kay! Oh!" She began to put her fiddle away.

"But aren't you pleased? I should be wild."

"Pleased? Oh yes, it is very kind of him; only I rather wish he had not come till the end of the term."

And then she smiled to herself as, smoothing her hair, she recollected the very first time he had come to call on her, and had found her making pies. How much had come and gone since then! The smile ended in a sigh.

"Now you look scrumptious. Dearest, if it is the great Mr. Kay, you will let me come in and have a glimpse at him, won't you? May I come in in about twenty minutes? I will cough loud outside the door."

Jenifer laughed heartily. "You need not take that precaution, I assure you. Gretchen was drawing on her imagination when she told you he had come from England on purpose to see me. What nonsense! No, come in with me now, and I will introduce you."

She drew her friend into the drawing-room with her, and she was glad she had done so, for when she met Kay's eyes, and felt the clasp of his hand, she was no longer so very sure that he had not come solely for her sake, though certainly, if he had, he was little likely to make Gretchen his confidante.

It was a year and a half since she had seen him, nor had she been home once in all that time. When she went away it was taken for granted that, though the distance was too great for her to come home in winter, the long summer holiday would release her. But when last summer came, Nicolai had said to her—

"If you go home now, you will lose in the six

weeks all you have gained in the last six months. Yes, yes, I know you are home-sick; but can't you bring that sacrifice to art?"

"Do you want me to stay alone and practise all the while the Conservatoire is shut up?" asked poor Jenifer, choking, as she thought of the sheets of purple foxglove and the forests of bracken all over the cliff top, and the great blue sea heaving up against the crags.

"No, no. I am a hard task-master, I know; but I am not quite such an ogre as that. This is my plan. I am taking a quartette party for a concert tour in Bavaria. Fraulein Waldstein was to have gone with me as second fiddle, but a sister of hers thinks fit to get married this summer, so she has failed me. I propose that you should take her place."

"I! Oh, mein Herr, I should be terrified! I am not fit."

"I think I am the best judge of that. You will not be frightened with me. And remember that with my pupils the word 'nervous' does not exist. It is expunged altogether out of the dictionary."

So Jenifer bowed to the master's iron will, and went. Her aunt and uncle wrote lamentable letters, but Nicolai was adamant; and Jenifer thanked him when she found that his plan had given her an insight into the practical work of her profession that years of study could never have done, and that under his powerful protection she had learned to face an audience with an absolute self-possession.

So, after her long absence, it was with an overwhelming mixture of feelings that she greeted Kay. She feared to seem too warm, yet he was a link with home; perhaps even he could bring news of Kerranstow by that "word of mouth" which is worth so many letters.

"Have you been at Kerranstow lately?" was her eager question as soon as greetings and introductions were disposed of.

"Have I not, indeed! Why, I come almost straight from there. You see, I knew the way to ensure myself a welcome."

The polite assurance of one for his own sake was not forthcoming, and she had so many questions to ask that they seemed to tumble over each other.

"Yes, I went to see your people just before I started," he said in answer to one of them, trying to frame his replies in the order of her desires. "Mr. Lyon is looking as hearty as ever, not a day older, and both he and your aunt were brimming over with messages—love and reproaches for staying away so long; and there would have been cream, too, if there had been any hope of its standing the journey in this warm weather. No, I was not staying at my old quarters; my good Peninah has got a 'permanent gentleman'—a little off his head, I believe. She was deeply afflicted at not being able to receive me. I was staying at the

Vicarage. Dear old Septimus sent his love, and I am to write him a long letter when I have heard you play."

"And John Yeo?"

"Ah yes, to be sure. John sent his duty and respects. He could talk of nothing but you the whole way when he drove me to meet the coach. He distinguished himself greatly last winter at the wreck of the *Osprey*—but you will have heard all about that."

"So poor Mr. Dendron is dead? How terribly sudden it must have been! How is Letty?"

He shrugged his shoulders a little. "Poor little soul! It must have been a great shock to her, of course, and I fancy she misses poor Dendron more than she expected; but she is an enigma. The first time I saw her on a Sunday in her weeds I thought she looked very disconsolate, but when I went to call I found her capless, playing tennis with her brother-in-law."

"Ah well!" said Jenifer, charitably, "it is nearly four months, you know; and Letty was always one of those who throw things off quickly. She is not alone, I suppose?"

"No, a sister and baby nephew had been there some time, and Sir Edward Travers had just gone down when I was there. She told me she meant to go abroad with them for part of the summer. I expect, after this autumn, Kerranstow will see her no more."

"I am almost surprised she stayed so long. I wonder what she will do?"

"Marry again, I expect, after a decent time has elapsed. Did you hear that Dendron's mines have weathered the crisis, and are paying very well again? She is a rich woman now. He has been very generous; everything is left to her absolutely."

Jenifer's first hunger for news being appeased, she began to ask him of his own doings. The papers had kept her informed of his professional successes, and she did not forget to congratulate him on the purchase of "Barren Toil" for the nation by the Chantry Bequest. He was now on his way to Bavaria, he told her.

"Rather a long way round," put in Mina, who had felt herself hitherto somewhat out of it; the old friends had had so much to say in which she could take no part.

"Not when one can see a friend by a slight detour, mein Fräulein," was his courteous response. "I mean to dawdle through some of the less known towns—Würzburg, Ratisbon, perhaps Bamberg," he pursued. "I am afraid of getting too narrow and *maniéré* if I stick too closely to one range of subjects. I intend to do a series of studies there; perhaps pitch my tent and paint a picture, if anything draws me very strongly."

"Shall you stay in Wimmelhahn long?" queried Mina, who was nothing if not inquisitive.

"That depends——" He looked at Jenifer, and his eyes finished the sentence—on you.

It made her nervous, and she hastily changed the subject by inquiring whether he had seen the lions of Wimmelhahn. It appeared he had, but was more than willing to see them all over again in their company. Then Frau Klieschmann came upon the scene, full of hospitable invitations. Finally it was arranged that he should escort the whole party to an open-air concert next evening, where they were to be his guests at supper; and he departed, leaving Mina in doubt whether to be most disappointed at his plainness or most ecstatic at having talked to so eminent a painter.

When he was gone, Jenifer went back to her practising, and girded at herself for losing her place and wholly forgetting whether she had practised her study in thirds or not.

Certainly we English are deplorably behindhand in the matter of amusing ourselves. It is not easy, out of London, to hear good music at all, and then it means a costly ticket, evening dress, and two hours shut up in a hot room. Our Continental neighbours, especially the Germans, understand far better wherein enjoyment consists. Hardly a town of any pretension but has its concerts "im Freie," where, in pleasant surroundings, an excellent band discourses sweet music, while the listeners stroll about at will, or sit in little parties round small tables and enjoy coffee, ices, or supper, according to their tastes, at prices that would make the hair of Spiers and Pond curl with horror.

At Wimmelhahn the concert-place was a wide clearing in the midst of a grove of lime-trees, whose fragrance was heavy on the summer dusk. Just round the band-stand and the little tables was a ring of lamps, interspersed with Chinese lanterns and strings of those pretty little coloured lights that are like tinted glow-worms. No rude and garish electric light marred the effect, but beyond the circle the wood was left in the semi-obscurity of the moonlight; and below, mysterious little pathways meandered down to the shores of the lake.

Denis Kay and his three guests had finished their little repast, and were chatting in the pauses of the music. Presently the band began to play the march from "Tannhäuser," and Denis leant forward and said to Jenifer—

"Won't you come for a little stroll with me?"

She was playing with her programme, creasing it up into the semblance of a fan, and for a moment she did not answer; then she said—

"I think not, thanks. I am a little tired, and it is very nice here."

The music by this time had wrought itself into a fine frenzy, and under cover of it he said—

"Very well; as you please; but will you let me see you to-morrow some time—alone?"

For answer she quietly rose from her place, and, as they moved away, he said to Frau Klieschmann—

"Miss Lyon and I are just going to take a little turn round. We shall not be long. We shall find you still here?"

Jenifer's chaperone nodded a good-natured acquiescence, and they walked side by side down one of the narrow paths that were less thronged, away from the lights and the music. He did not begin to speak at once; while the loud, triumphant march was in progress it was impossible to say anything in a low tone, and Jenifer, feeling from his decided manner how much was meant by this walk, left him to begin in his own way. She would not hamper him by any attempts at ordinary conversation, and she felt that any effort to turn him aside would be thrown away; he must have his say.

He waited till they were standing by the lake. The music came softly now, and it seemed to help him to speak better than silence could have done.

"Forgive me if I am too persistent. I am afraid your not wishing to come with me seems as if you meant not to give me any hope; but I could not take my answer till I had a chance to put my question."

She had wished to spare him a useless avowal, but to say so seemed to take too much for granted. She held her peace.

"I think I have been very patient," he went on; "it is nearly two years since I spoke to you first. And now I want to tell you I have not changed at all; have you?"

"No," said Jenifer, low but very steadily. "I am very sorry, but I cannot say anything but 'No.'"

"You are very steadfast; but surely you don't mean to devote your whole life to a remembrance?"

"What?" she put in, in a puzzled tone. "I don't understand!"

"I could not help guessing," he said, "that when I asked you before, the place that I coveted was preoccupied; but now that he is dead, poor fellow——"

"Dead!"

He could not see her face in the uncertain moonlight, but the tone of her voice frightened him.

"I ought not to have reminded you so suddenly, so roughly," he cried penitently. "I was a brute to do it. Forgive me."

"Reminded me? But I did not know—I had never heard—oh, tell me!"

For a moment he thought that the agitation of a cruelly sudden reminder must have unhinged her brain; then the possibility of a blunder began to dawn on him. While he paused dismayed, she, gathering her scattered wits, bethought her of a perplexing warning he had once given her, and with lightning quickness saw the mistake she had been betrayed into. She gave a sigh of relief.

"Oh, I see; you were speaking of my poor cousin Fred. I remember now your seeming once to fancy that I cared for him in that sort of way; but it was all your fancy. I was fond of him, but not like that."

It was his turn now to be perplexed and utterly at sea. What could she mean? Who could she have thought he was speaking of? But not for worlds would he have betrayed that he was aware of the implied admission.

"I was a blundering idiot," he said. "I have frightened you." For indeed she was still white and shaky. "Come and sit down for a few minutes."

She let him find her a quiet seat in the secluded walk that skirted the lake. As he seated himself beside her he could still hear her breath coming in a quick, panting way, and the hand that rested on her knee trembled. He forbore to pursue his cause just then, but asking her permission with a gesture, rolled and lighted a cigarette. He could not have shown greater tact, and she inwardly thanked him for it, for while he was so occupied, the silence that she needed did not feel irksome.

He, too, was agitated; he felt as if he had just stumbled against an unsuspected obstacle, and had lost his bearings. As the soothing fragrance of the friendly tobacco floated about him, his thoughts began to disentangle themselves. He was no nearer his goal than he had been two years ago; that was very evident. He had invented for himself such an entirely satisfactory story, that he forgot on what slender grounds it rested. She loved her worthless cousin, and would not give him up; the cousin was providentially removed; she would fret at first, of course, but the wound would heal, and she would turn to the man who had had such long patience, and kept true to her for four years. And now, behold, it was a dream! If the obstacle were a chimera, so, too, was the clearing it away: the barrier was still to seek, and, whatever it was, he feared it was as strong as ever. Clearly her horrified exclamation bore some personal meaning, and it must needs refer to some one who belonged to the days in which he had loved her first. There were not so many men at Kerranstow that the choice was difficult. He was perplexed. He had never suspected anything between those two, and yet—he remembered the shipwreck, and Jenifer going out alone upon the rocks to watch the rescue. Well, he supposed there was no hope for him; but he must make sure, else he would never have any peace. He took the cigarette from his lips.

"May I go on?" he asked.

She looked down. "I wish you would not; it is not any use."

"Very well. So be it."

He rose, and tossed away the half-burnt cigarette into the bushes. The impassioned appeal he had imagined himself making to her died down like a slaked fire. After all, if she could not love him, he did not want to induce her to marry him. He felt bitter and angry with her, with himself, with fate. She felt that her refusal to hear him had been curt, and added—

"I shall never marry. I am married to my fiddle."

"Pshaw! Have I not my art, and does that hinder my wanting you? Do you suppose, if I married, I should leave off painting?"

"No, no, of course not; but men are different. I don't want to give a divided allegiance."

At that moment two men passed them, and one, turning his head, with a long, scrutinizing glance at Jenifer, took off his hat. The moon, which shone out for a moment, lighted up a hook nose and brilliant black eyes. Kay looked after him, and when he was out of hearing, asked rather sharply—

"Who is that? and why does he stare at you in that censorious way?"

"That is my violin master, Herr Nicolai."

"Is that the fellow who would not let you go home last summer? Is it at his dictation you are resolving to give up a real human life, and vowing yourself to your violin as though it were a vocation? If I thought that, I would win you from it yet."

"No, no!" she cried; "I chose my career freely, and unbiased by anybody. He has nothing to do with it, except that he helps me to make it worth while."

"I cannot understand your point of view," pursued Denis. "I am a worker myself, and I know what it is to devote one's self with passion to attaining one's goal; but to me my work would not be less, but more, for having you beside me: you would complete and broaden my life on every side. Why should it not be the same with you?"

"Because of the one thing lacking," she said; "because I cannot answer the love you are offering."

"Ay, I knew it. It is there that the real hitch lies.

> "'Had you loved me once, as you have not loved;
> Had the chance been with us that has not been,'"

he quoted under his breath. "Well, I suppose you cannot help it. I am not going to cry for mercy."

He turned away, and fixed his eyes upon the lake, while he was trying to grapple with the conviction that he was defeated once for all, and that it was idle to lull himself with the hope that he might yet have another chance. He saw, without seeing, the long, wavering reflections of the lights of the town upon the other shore, and the curving line of the old arched bridge with its statues across the narrow neck of the lake. He even noted how the broken mirrors were repeated and repeated, larger and larger, till they were lost in the tall rushes by the bank. He had succeeded in so many ambitions, and now the one thing he had chosen to set all his heart upon, and which would have made the rest worth while, was denied him. In a minute or two he came back to Jenifer.

"Then it must be good-bye," he said; "and good-bye for a long while. I shall be on my road again to-morrow early. Now shall we go back to the others?"

And almost in silence they retraced their steps.

CHAPTER III.

RACHEL TREBY was drinking tea at Pencoet. Since Oliver's death she and Letty had drawn together again. For some time after Alick's departure there had been a coldness; for Rachel, woman-like, had blamed Mrs. Dendron far more than she did her brother, and had kept away severely to mark her disapproval; but now Letty's loss had drawn a veil over the past; pity and sympathy had stepped in, and bygones were bygones. In the scarcity of neighbours, neither could afford to dispense with the other's company, and both were glad to let the breach close without a word of explanation.

Letty, somewhat to the surprise of her friends, had chosen to stay on at Pencoet, though Mr. Jaques had offered at once to release her from the year for which the house was still on her hands. She knew that in her deep mourning she should be a *gêne* in her mother's house, and till she could decently go about and amuse herself like other people, she preferred to keep her own home in the country. Mrs. Brabazon, having settled Lady Travers to her mind, had the twins to present this season, but Violet was under a temporary cloud, having bestowed her affections upon a younger son, and as she showed a more obstinate disposition than her elder sister had done, was better out of the way for the present; so Letty might have her to beguile her solitude as much as she pleased. The two sisters had been quietly happy together, and beyond taking off her cap to play tennis, Letty had done nothing to scandalize the neighbourhood. She had spent a good deal of the autumn abroad with Sir Edward and Lady Travers, and now she had Violet with her again. She was getting restless, however, and was beginning to talk of Italy or the south of France before the cold weather should set in; the *rôle* of disconsolate widow, prettily as she had played it, was beginning to pall upon her; she wanted to be amused, still more perhaps to be admired.

They had been discussing plans and projects over the tea-cups, to the envy of Rachel, tied at home as she was from year's end to year's end, with all her eager desire to see foreign countries and improve her mind, stifled under a dreary round of parish activities.

"Ah, don't tantalize me," she cried, as Letty flung down a Baedeker, out of which she had been reading tempting bits. "You make me feel quite wicked, when you talk of Florence and the Pitti Palace."

"It is too bad. I wish you could come with us. Well, let us change the subject. Tell me about Jenifer; I was so sorry to miss her in the summer. Is she altered?"

"On the surface she is; she has grown very dignified and self-possessed, but in reality she is as simple as ever, and she was so happy to be at home again."

"And her playing?"

"It is really wonderful. I must own I thought Mr. Jaques was making a mistake in sending her there. I fancied she was too old to begin a professional training, and it was a pity to let her waste time over it when she might have been earning for herself; but it has been worth while; she will do great things."

"Mr. Jaques must be pleased."

"Pleased! He is perfectly wild over her, and so is John Yeo. She gave a concert in the tithe-barn, and invited all the village, and it was rich to see not only John but the two Polsues bursting with pride and admiration. Next year she leaves the Conservatoire, and then she hopes to play in England."

With Nicolai to back her, she ought to do well," said Letty. "I wonder if she will get any good London engagements. Fancy that little slip of a girl! Well, I always thought there was good stuff in her."

"It is a pity she does not come home for the winter holidays," said Violet, coming round to the fireside. "It really seems a shame of us to go away and leave you all alone. There actually won't be a soul left in the place."

"Except Mrs. Twisselton," laughed Letty. "Rachel, I believe, when we get back, we shall find that you have been goaded by sheer solitude into a bosom friendship with her. You'll be calling her dear Louisa."

"Never," cried Rachel, laughing; "besides, I hope I shall have Alick to save me from such a fate as that."

"Oh," said Letty, looking up with some show of interest, "is Mr. Studland coming back? You never told me you expected him."

"Didn't I? Well, we always knew this winter would bring him. I have not had a letter for ages; but I saw by the papers that the *Impregnable* sailed last week. I hope she will be paid off by Christmas."

"I wonder I did not notice; but the *Times* has been so deadly dull lately, I have only skimmed it in the most superficial way. I am very glad you will have somebody to cheer your solitude."

"You will just miss him, if you start early in December," said Rachel, rather anxious to see if her news had any effect on Letty's plans.

"So I shall," was the unconcerned rejoinder. "Well, I dare say he will not be going any long voyage again at present, so we may meet some other time."

"No, I think he expects to be appointed to the Channel Squadron. After such a long spell of foreign service, they never send a man off directly, so he will be at Portsmouth for some time."

Soon after, Rachel took her leave and went away, thinking to herself, "How very wise of Letty to be out of the way just at first. After all the talk there was, it would be very unseemly to begin flirting again, and it will not be a year till February. But I suppose that is how it will end. I am sorry; but one cannot choose for other people."

"Letty," said Violet, when she was gone, "I have been thinking that if we were to start a week earlier, and go first to Baveno——"

"I am not by any means sure that I shall start before Christmas at all," said Letty, staring into the fire.

"Not start before Christmas? Why, you said just now you could not stand another English Christmas in the country."

"My dear, you should never remind people of what they said just now; it is bad form."

Violet shrugged her shoulders.

"I don't think I would change, if I were you," she said.

"What do you know about it?"

There was a minute's silence. Then Letty suddenly burst out—

"Violet, what would you say to throwing up

Italy, and going off to St. Petersburg to skate? You know I have always had a wild desire to see Russia."

"Letty!"

"No, of course, I know it is impossible and visionary—and if it were not, I would not do it for ten thousand worlds."

She rose as she spoke, and, taking a candle, went up to dress for dinner. Upstairs she lingered over the fire.

"I really cannot see," she said to herself, "why I am to flee from the face of Alick Studland as if I were afraid or ashamed to meet him. I could see that Rachel was mentally patting me on the back for going, and thinking it a most virtuous step, whereas it was purely accidental. My plans are not like the law of the Medes and Persians, which altereth not. If I choose to stay a week or so, and see him, pray why shouldn't I?"

"So you are not going quite so soon?" said Rachel, some days later, meeting the sisters.

"No," answered Letty, composedly; we had to put it off. It was rather a bore as it has turned so cold; but my great object was to be at Florence at the same time as the Vincent Briggs, and I have just heard they cannot get away till January."

Mrs. Twisselton called on Rachel a week or so before Mr. Studland's expected arrival.

"Ah," said she, sagaciously, "I thought Mrs. Dendron would not go to Italy when she heard your brother was expected back. She will not go at all, you may depend upon it."

"Really, Mrs. Twisselton," said Rachel, with righteous indignation, "I should think that under her circumstances Mrs. Dendron might be safe from remarks of that kind."

But she was provoked with Letty for putting it in the power of her neighbours to say that she had postponed her going on purpose. Mrs. Twisselton was a person uncommonly difficult to abash; she saw that Miss Treby was annoyed, but instead of changing the subject, pursued—

"Oh well, you know, I think it is absurd to pretend to ignore what we are all so perfectly well aware of. He evidently comes home because he knows she is free, and it would be ridiculous in her to run away."

"You are quite mistaken; it is nothing of the kind. His ship is ordered home, and of course he comes here."

"After all," pursued Mrs. Twisselton, serenely, "I don't see that there is anything to be annoyed about. She is free now, and not only that, but if report speaks true, rich as well. She would be quite a catch for him. Do tell me, is it true that her husband positively left her his money absolutely, whether she married again or not?"

"I really cannot tell you. I never inquire into what does not concern me."

And with this crushing rejoinder, Rachel at last managed to stamp out the conversation.

The churchyard at Kerranstow, after morning service, was the best place in the parish for a casual encounter between two people who wished to meet without the formality of a call. Alick Studland had forsaken Hennacombe the first Sunday after his arrival, and walked over to Kerranstow, either for this reason, or because Mr. Jaques's terse, original, and vigorous discourses suited him better than his step-father's well-worn platitudes, which he found always exercised rather a soporific effect.

Just beyond the lych-gate lay a narrow space of common land intersected by worn footpaths leading to the various stiles that afforded short cuts to the outlying farms. Here little groups were wont to assemble to exchange greetings, comment on the weather, or hear or tell the news. Such parishioners as drove, waited here for their vehicles to be fetched from the inn at the top of the hill where they were put up; and here it was natural enough for Studland to greet Mrs. Dendron.

He was a trifle nervous, being intensely conscious of the circumstances under which he had last parted from her, and feeling or fancying the eyes of the whole congregation upon him; but he need not have been anxious; Letty was fully equal to the occasion. She gave him her hand, smiled graciously while she asked how he had prospered on the homeward voyage, and whether he had escaped the recent gales in the Bay of Biscay; and then introducing him to her sister, walked on towards the high-road with Mrs. Twisselton, leaving him to follow with Violet or take his leave just as he pleased.

Not Studland himself, nor even her lynx-eyed companion could have told that she had the faintest recollection of anything beyond mere acquaintanceship having ever been between them. Clearly she intended him to see that the past was past. If there was ever to be any renewal of interest, it must be begun all over again.

He walked with Violet up to the corner where their roads parted, and left her there, raising his hat to her sister who just turned round and smiled a distant farewell.

She was still wearing her widow's weeds, and with them she had assumed something of an appropriate manner. As a child, her sisters had said of her, "Letty always behaves according to what she has on," and their shrewdness was not far wrong. It was not that she affected any sentimental grief or dejection which every one who knew her would have known she must be far from feeling, but there was an air of soberness—a gentle gravity and decorum in her demeanour that went well with the little white border inside her bonnet, the snowy muslin cuffs and crinkly crape.

There was hardly an eye among the little congregation that did not follow them with some degree of interest, nor a tongue but had some comment to make.

Peninah paused in an ungraceful attitude with

one foot on one side of the stile and one on the other that she might not lose a detail of the meeting.

"He be gooin' after her," she said, in an excited whisper to Grace; and after a minute's pause occupied in getting her whole person to the further side of the stile, she added, "They du meet uncommon cool, surely."

"Ah," responded Grace, "and see now, he is walkin' with the young lady and not wi' she, after all. Ah wud'n be surprised now if she misses un. Maybe she was too forthcomin'. You mind the old sayin'—'The fruit that will fall without shakin' is not worth the takin.'"

Septimus, too, was watching; he had lingered to see if Alick would come in and have lunch with him; but perceiving how he was occupied, turned aside to his own door.

"I suppose there is little doubt how that will end," he said to himself. "People might say it is rather soon; but under the circumstances I don't know that anybody could blame her. There is a great deal of good in her; with a man she loved, she would make a charming wife."

CHAPTER IV.

WHAT everybody expects has a habit of coming to pass; not so much from the remarkable sagacity of "everybody" as because a certain kind of prediction has a tendency to bring about its own fulfilment; much as one has seen a solid mahogany table—on which has been brought to bear the expectation, otherwise faith, of some half-dozen people—revolve in accordance with their desires, and soberly waltz away. Only on the more sensitive human soul the pressure of finger-tips is not required.

With the new year Letty had changed her mourning, and of course everybody knew what that portended. If she had been bent on carrying out her widowhood to its full limits, she would have worn her bonnet till the end of February, the month in which she had lost her husband; but then, as Mrs. Twisselton observed, Mr. Studland would have been away, and where would have been the use of tacitly declaring herself ready to entertain new proposals. She was still in black, but the crape had vanished, and the widow's bonnet was replaced by a frivolous little felt hat. Grace Yeo noticed the transformation, and so did Peninah.

Violet, too, drew her own conclusions when the box of hats arrived from Madame Marie, and her sister consulted her as to the most becoming shape. Letty's family, as has already been mentioned, were in the habit of predicting her line of conduct from the indications of her dress, and she too thought that a change of costume setting in at such an unpropitious time of year could not be without significance.

"I don't believe we shall go to Italy after all," she said, with apparent irrelevance, when the prettiest hat had been selected and the others laid aside.

"Oh, I don't know; perhaps we may. Shall you be very much disappointed if we don't? You know I am very fond of making vague projects, but I hate being tied down to definite plans. It was one of poor Oliver's trying peculiarities that he always expected one to make up one's mind definitely beforehand, and adhere rigidly to one's choice. I don't know that I feel inclined to start this month."

Then Violet went straight to the point.

"You are in a great hurry to give up your liberty again, Letty. I should not be if I were you; you have plenty of money now, and nobody's leave to ask in the spending of it. Why should you be so anxious to put your neck under the yoke again before you have had any fun?"

"I don't know, I am sure. But I have by no means made up my mind to do anything of the sort."

"Perhaps not," said Violet, astutely; "but I can see you have made up your mind that somebody shall ask you to."

"Ah, that is another question altogether."

"It may be; but you can never tell how that may end."

"You have grown very wise for your years, little sister; but you don't know all the ins and outs of this case, and I don't know, I am sure, whether I could explain them to you. He was here invalided once about two years ago, and he and I saw a good deal of each other, and got to be rather friends. You would think there couldn't be enough people here to gossip, but they contrive to do it somehow, and the upshot was that he took fright—and flight. There was not a grain of harm in it; we were friends; *voilà tout;* but since he chose to put that complexion on it by running away, why, now that I am free—don't you see?"

"No, I don't see at all. I think you are very silly—unless you care for him."

"I never said I did not care for him. I think I do a little sometimes."

"I don't believe you do. I wish you would let the whole thing slide, and go off to Italy."

"Perhaps I will, by-and-by. I am only waiting on events."

Violet was silent a minute or two; then she suddenly asked—

"Do you ever hear from Philip Latimer, Letty?"

"Never. Don't be romantic, Vi. I am going into the other room to write letters."

She went into the library, and took out her writing-case and a lawyer's letter that demanded an answer; but she did not begin to write; she sat biting the end of her pen and musing, not on the pros and cons of a certain investment he had recommended to her notice, but on the conversation she had just had with her sister.

"Violet has a great deal of shrewdness," she said to herself; "but no one can decide for any one else in a question of this sort."

Neither did she find it so very easy to decide it for herself. It was not a question of right and wrong that troubled her; that is one that can always be decided when approached with sincerity; but she was in doubt which way her own desires really lay. She knew very well she should feel affronted if Studland went away without any effort to avail himself of the altered position of affairs; she knew she was drawing up again the ravelled threads of influence, and that it lay more with her now than with him whether he should speak or be silent; she also knew that she could not draw him on to speak and then deny him, without a breach of her code of honour, whatever she might pretend to Violet; and yet on the question whether she really wanted to marry him or not, she could say neither yea or nay. As she said just now, she must wait upon events.

As to Alick, he was waiting upon events too; but his uncertainty was rather as to what he ought to do. On the one hand was the doubt how far he stood committed by previous entanglements—a feeling strengthened by the evident expectations of the bystanders; and on the other the fear of laying himself open to the imputation of fortune hunting.

It is curious when one reflects upon real life, and leaves the presumptions of fiction out of account, how very large a proportion of marriages are decided on side issues rather than on the main factor of personal feeling.

He almost wished he had not come home just now. He had not thought to find Letty still at Kerranstow, or perhaps he would not have ventured himself again in the sphere of her fascinations. It was one thing to slide into a pleasant flirtation to while away a long summer holiday; it was quite another to turn it into a lifelong decision. He was not a weak man in the ordinary sense, but where a woman is concerned, Samson may find himself at fault, and on this matter he felt as though he were blundering in a fog. He wished he had a clearer recollection of how far he had gone—further than he intended or realized at the time, he feared, to judge by the expectant attitude, not only of the local gossips, but even of Septimus Jaques himself, on whose judgment singularly unbiased and clear, he had great reliance. Only could Septimus fathom the mind of a woman — such a woman as Letty Dendron?

On just that crucial question of what Letty felt or expected Alick might be pardoned if he found himself completely in the dark. Her indifference to poor Oliver was indeed an open secret; but whether the preference she showed himself had been a real affection or only an idle sentiment to solace an empty heart, he could not tell, and certainly would not know till he asked her—if then.

As to his own heart—*pace* the romantic reader, usually of the softer sex and of tender age, whose devout faith is that to love once is to love for ever—it did not follow that because he had been very much in love last October two years, that he should be so in this present January. Quick fires burn out quick, and a few months after he left Kerranstow the episode had become merely a pensive remembrance. Yet he could not be with her much and not feel a reviving tenderness; she was just as pretty and more winning than ever, with the greater softness which a touch of penitence, as well as freedom from the strain of difficult relations had given to her manner. In old days she was more capricious and sometimes cynical. She satisfied his taste as she had always done, but he wanted more than that; he wanted a sense of perfect confidence that he knew he should never feel in her. In a sense she was an enigma to him; and though there may be a piquant charm in making love to an enigma, when it comes to marrying the case is not quite the same.

He might have kept away, but to do so in such a place as Kerranstow, where neighbours were so few and so dependent on each other, would have been an extreme step which he felt he had no right to take, so he visited at Pencoet, sometimes with his sister and sometimes without; Violet's presence there making it quite natural and proper that he should do so.

If it was any one's doing, it was Rachel's; the very person of all others who, if she could have had her way, would have liked to prevent its happening altogether. She could not put the probability out of her head, could not hinder herself from watching his manner to Letty when they were together, or looking as if she expected some news every time he came back from Pencoet. She and Mrs. Twisselton at least had decided which way the table was to spin.

So the day came, as it was bound to come sooner or later, when he went into the gates between the stone griffins a free man, and came out trothplight to the widow. It was a little thing that brought it to pass. Letty had done something foolish about her dividends—signed something she ought not to have signed, and had had a very scolding letter from her trustee. Clever as she was, she was a little apt to blunder and be tiresome about business, chiefly from not doing as she was bid, but she always resented being found fault with. The two sisters had promised to go and help Rachel with a Mothers' Tea that afternoon, but Letty was upset about her letter, so Violet went alone.

Alick, calling in the late afternoon, found Letty solitary and fretting. She unburdened her trouble to him, and asked his advice in that confiding way that appeals to most men. The result was a foregone conclusion. It is hardly needful to go into detail; the scene can be so well understood. All his chivalrous compassion was roused on her behalf; he could not bear to see her bullied and unhappy. She genuinely felt the need of somebody to be good to her and take her part, and quite forgot her intention to let him wait her pleasure for his answer and keep him dangling for his good and to punish him for his want of alacrity. She yielded at once, and let him comfort her and assure her that she should never be bothered about business again; he would keep every rough wind from blowing on her.

She would not let him stay till Violet came in; she preferred to have time to tell her own story in her own way. She was not at all sure she could count on her sister's approval; not that Violet did not like Alick, quite the contrary; but she evidently feared lest Letty might be too precipitate, and make an irreparable mistake a second time. At any rate, it would be easier if she were able to pave the way for her confession.

After seeing him out, she came back to the warm, dimly lighted drawing-room, and sitting down on her heels on the hearthrug, wondered at the new development of her affairs. It had come upon her suddenly. If any one had told her when she got up that morning she would be engaged to Alick Studland before night, she certainly would not have believed the rash prediction. She had not even made up her mind that she would accept him at all, and assuredly it was never part of her programme to do so directly she was asked; but he had a masterful way with him that bore down her hesitations, and she found she had said "yes" while she was debating whether it should be "no" or "wait a little."

"I think I shall be very happy," she said to herself. "He is very different to poor Oliver. He is wonderfully tender and good to one if one is in trouble. I hope he won't be overbearing; I went down like a reed before him this afternoon. I wonder if he is very much in love with me. Sometimes I think he is, and then again I am not quite sure. He certainly was, and will be again. At any rate, it will be my own fault if he isn't. And now to face Violet."

Meanwhile Alick, after he had parted with his betrothed at the hall door, had an odd sort of feeling as if he had stepped out of Armida's garden into the cold, damp, prosaic night. He stopped a minute in the shelter of one of the stone griffins to try and get a light for his pipe, but the wind was gusty, and match after match went out. He shivered a little and drew up the collar of his coat as he swore a small oath, and then laughed at himself for feeling cross at such a trifle. "By all laws of romance," he thought, "I ought not to know that it is cold, or even whether my pipe is in or out; but alas! the raptures that are appropriate at twenty are not forthcoming when one is nearer forty. Those blessed matches must be damp."

He trudged on, but at the corner where the Pencoet lane met the high-road he saw a friendly spark approaching, which his keen sailor eyes soon discovered to belong to a lean, stooping figure and a slouched hat.

"Hullo, parson, will you give us a light?"

Septimus stopped till he came up.

"Oh, it is you, Alick, is it? And I need hardly ask where you are coming from."

Studland waited to answer till his pipe was drawing satisfactorily, and when that important business was concluded, he said drily—

"No, you need not, and in future no one need trouble themselves to count how many times I go to Pencoet; it will probably be pretty often while I am here. Mrs. Dendron has just promised to make me a happy man at Easter."

"Dear old fellow! I am so sincerely glad. I can only say I hope you will be as happy as you deserve." He held out his hand.

"Thanks."

"You must let me apologize," went on Mr. Jaques, "for my ill-timed pleasantry just now. You know I would never watch your comings and goings in any inquisitive spirit, but it was impossible to help feeling an interest and a hope that things were coming right for you at last."

"I know. I am afraid I was a bit crusty. You must own the subject has had a good deal of unnecessary handling."

"To be sure. Well, well, I don't know when anything has pleased me more."

Alick did not respond. He could not have told why, but it annoyed him to have his engagement looked on as in any sense the reward of merit. He was so sure that Rachel would take that view, and probably be more outspoken in stating it even than the vicar, that he was rather unwilling to meet her, and felt it as a reprieve when the latter said—

"Come home and dine with me, won't you? I believe Miss Treby has some function or other on to-night; you won't get anything but a meat tea if you go home, if that."

He accepted gladly, and the two friends spent a pleasant evening together, talking over life on a man-of-war on the China seas, the little politics of the village, or the greater politics of St. Stephen's

—anything, in short, but Alick's engagement, which was not once mentioned between them.

Probably one reason why men's friendships are as a rule, if less vivid, more durable than women's, is this faculty they have for letting a subject alone. No one could have felt a keener sympathy than Septimus, but so soon as he perceived, as he very quickly did, that Alick for some reason or other was shy of entering on the topic, he at once let it drop, and refrained from betraying the smallest interest. The fact in no way disturbed his idea of its entire satisfactoriness; Alick was not an expansive man, nor was he at an expansive age. A young lover might be expected to enjoy nothing so much as dilating on his good fortune; but it appeared natural enough that Studland should keep his raptures to himself and prefer to talk of other matters with his old friend.

It was not to be a long engagement, for there was nothing to wait for. Studland, though not a commander yet, would probably soon get his promotion; but there was no need to wait for that since Letty professed herself perfectly content with his modest position, and was sufficiently well-endowed through poor Oliver's liberality. The wedding, therefore, was fixed for April, and in the meanwhile Alick would be at Portsmouth, leaving Letty free to devote her mind to the important question of trousseau.

Wedding garments not being obtainable at Kerranstow, or even at Bridesworth in accordance with Letty's requirements, she spent most of the intervening time in town; but since Alick had a strong wish to be married by Septimus in Kerranstow Church, and hated the idea of a gay London wedding, she decided the affair should take place from her own house, and her mother and sisters were to come down to her a few days beforehand.

CHAPTER V.

"JOHN, I have some news for you," said Mr. Jaques, coming out into the stable-yard, where old Blanche was undergoing her morning toilet. He had an open letter in his hand, for the post was just in, and the man who had brought it was at that moment being regaled on bread and cheese and a glass of home-brewed in the kitchen, according to custom, while waiting for the outgoing mail. "Miss Jenifer is in England again; more than that, she is coming west to play at some concerts, and soon after Easter she expects to be at Roscorla."

John stopped hissing at Blanche, who looked round in mild surprise at the cessation of the accustomed noise, and pausing with currycomb in his hand, said—

"Miss Jenifer! God bless her! Why, I'd walk forty mile any day to hear her play her fiddle again."

His master drew out a pink paper enclosed in the letter, and held it out to him.

"See here; she has sent me the programme of a concert at Exeter, where she is going to play next week. I mean to go and hear her, and I will take you with me. We will drive to Polesworthy and take the train, and we must put up in Exeter for the night."

John's weather-beaten face wrinkled up with pleasure till his little, twinkling eyes were nearly lost; then he only said—

"Thankye, sir; much obliged, I am sure."

At that moment Studland appeared. Intimates were very apt to find their way down to the Vicarage by the back lane; it was so much the most direct. Mr. Jaques turned to him eagerly.

"Will you come with me to Exeter on Tuesday, Alick, to hear Jenifer Lyon play? That is, if Mrs. Dendron can spare you."

Alick laughed. "Oh yes, she'll spare me fast enough; in fact, I think she will be rather glad to get rid of me. She has her head full of fashion-books of all sorts and sizes, and I am for ever mixing piles of patterns. I am to take her up to town the end of the week before I go back to my ship, but I could very well go on Tuesday. But how comes it that Miss Lyon is in England now? I thought she had to go on at the Conservatoire till the summer."

"Why, it appears there has been fighting at Wimmelhahn. Nicolai, her master, who, I should imagine, belongs to the *genus irritabile*, has quarrelled with the authorities, and thrown up his appointment; and Jenifer, I suppose, has ranged herself under his banner. At any rate, he, having come to London, has got her an engagement in this concert party, and has persuaded Frau Klieschmann to bring her, and let her make her *début* under his ægis at once. She is to play at Bath, Bristol, Exeter, and I don't know where beside; and then she hopes to get a little holiday at home while he looks out for something in London for her. He is such a powerful protector that I don't see that she could do better; she seems to be making a very good start for such a young thing."

"I am very glad to hear it. I shall like to hear her play again. Hers was the sort of playing that never bored one."

"It is a ballad concert, you understand; Madame Gianpietri, Signor Poldori, and so forth. However, she plays four times; twice in each part."

"Let them do their worst; it would be quite worth while going ten times the distance to hear her play once; wouldn't it, John?"

The Kerranstow party only reached Exeter in time to snatch a hasty dinner and hurry to the hall to get good places in the unreserved part. They had decided on this both to save the trouble of dressing and because they thought it best not to run the risk of embarrassing Jenifer by sitting in too conspicuous a part of the room, since they had not been able to let her know of their coming; in fact, up to the last minute the vicar had been uncertain on account of a sick parishioner. So they all sat together, John modestly behind his master.

They listened with an ungrateful impatience to Madame Gianpietri's fine bravura rendering of "Una Voce;" then came a vocal trio, and then Signor Poldori had his turn; but at last there was Jenifer in a white gown, tall and straight—the same Jenifer, yet different. Had she grown? or was it that the development of her figure, her stately carriage, and the way she had learned to hold her head made her look taller? One could hardly call her "little Jenifer" now. The little, thin arms of her teens had filled out into an exquisite shapeliness and grace, which the handling of her bow set off to great advantage. But for that she was hardly altered; just the same rich dark hair growing low about her forehead, and coiled in much the old way round her small head, and the same sea-colour in her eyes. She came on with a quiet grace and self-possession, and bowing to the audience, raised her violin to her chin and glanced over her shoulder at the accompanist. Her look went out over the whole room, but there was an unseeing expression in her eyes; they rested above the heads of the people, and remained fixed there; and Septimus, at least, was glad it was so, for he was a little anxious lest the sudden sight of her old friends might unsettle her composure. There was no danger; evidently she was wrapped up in the music. It was Beethoven's Romance in F; and as it went on, the listeners felt a growing sense of her power. Hackneyed it might be, but she knew how to draw out the full sense and breadth of emotion, so that it seemed to unfold new meanings, as a familiar chapter of the Bible will sometimes do, heard in the voice of a perfect reader.

As she bowed in acknowledgment of the cordial applause, Alick noticed that she glanced along the front rows as if in search of some one, and meeting the object she sought, gave him—or her, was it?—a little, satisfied smile as she moved away. He instantly conceived a sentiment of the most active dislike towards the recipient of that small, fine smile.

More vocal gymnastics, during which he could scarcely control his impatience. John Yeo, behind, applauded everything lustily, and was particularly impressed with the achievements of "Madam Jampastry," as he called the soprano. However, even repeated encores must come to an end at last, and it was not so very long before Jenifer stood before them again.

This time she was to play without notes, and there was no music-desk to intervene. As she stood a moment while the pianist was playing the prelude, her eyes wandered down the long room, and suddenly encountered the three familiar faces, all turned eagerly towards her. She started a little and changed colour, then she gave them a swift, bright smile of recognition, and drawing a long breath, as though to pull herself together, she broke into the brilliant rush of Bazzini's "Scherzo Fantastique."

No fear lest their presence had made her nervous; it seemed rather to have put her on her mettle. The audience could hardly believe that it was a mere girl who stood so quietly before them, hardly moving, only swaying a little, poised so lightly on her feet she looked as if a breath would blow her away, yet displaying such extraordinary mastery of her instrument. And it was not only the execution that was so marvellous; she carried her hearers away by the dash and fire with which she played. There was a perfect storm of applause at the end. Twice she came back and bowed; but the demand was too persistent. With a word to the accompanist, she looked and smiled at John Yeo, and began to play a charming little gipsy dance that he had taught her years ago in the old tithe-barn.

That time there was no clapping from John, and Alick, looking round, caught him furtively wiping his eyes on his coat-cuff.

A few minutes later, one of the men who had been selling programmes came and tapped Mr. Jaques on the arm.

"Miss Lyon's compliments, sir, and would you gentlemen please to step into the performers' room between the parts. Oh, and I was to say especially—John, too, if you please."

It was the regulation ten minutes' interval, and people were beginning to stand up to stretch their legs and exchange remarks, and some were going outside for a breath of fresh air or half a pipe, so they easily slipped out from their places and followed their conductor along a passage and up a narrow staircase at the back, into a little den behind the stage. It was a small room, and rather full. There was a table in the corner with refreshments, and round it the four vocalists were crowding with some friends who had come round from the front. "Madam Jampastry" was enjoying a glass of stout with her sandwiches, and there was a buzz of laughter and talking. For a moment they paused in the doorway, looking for a white figure, but Jenifer, who found the room draughty, was wrapped in a long grey cloak and a feather boa, and stood leaning on the corner of the mantelpiece. In a moment she turned and saw them, and setting down her coffee-cup, came towards them with a beaming face and both hands outstretched.

"Oh, Mr. Jaques, how good of you, how very good of you to come all this way to hear me play! But I am glad I did not know of it before, or I should have been nervous. I hope you were not dissatisfied?"

"Dissatisfied! My dear child, I am more than pleased; I am proud of you. You quite take my breath away."

"I am so glad. And now you must come and speak to Frau Klieschmann, whom you ought to know for Muriel's sake. You know, now Mina is married, she is so good as to come and take care of me."

For Mina had, in the end, bestowed her young affections, not on the tenor, nor on the blue-eyed Engelhardt, but on a thriving, middle-aged brewer in the new part of the town.

Jenifer turned back to Studland then, and said how glad she was to see Kerranstow so well represented, and asked for Rachel and his step-father. She had not resumed her glove, and as her hand lay an instant in his, he thought how cold it was; but not colder than her greeting. She looked round.

"But what have you done with John? where is he? Ah, there he is! Come in, John."

There was nothing chilly in the cordial handshake she gave her old friend.

"Oh, John, I was so pleased to see you! Did you think of the old lessons in the tithe-barn? I did. I played that gipsy dance on purpose for you. How is Grace? You must give my love to her when you go back. And Abel and Jeremiah, are they well? And do you still keep up the quartette practice? We will have some splendid ones when I come home for my holiday."

At that moment some one else entered the room —a slight, dark man, with a large expanse of shirt-front, and a gardenia in his button-hole. He came up to Jenifer and said something in a soft voice. It was in German, but it was evidently complimentary, to judge by the expression of his eyes and the gratified glow that sprang to her face; but she answered in English.

"I am so glad you thought so. I ought to do my best to-night, with so much encouragement. Mr. Jaques, this is my master, Herr Nicolai. He is on his way to Plymouth, and only think, he stopped here for this evening on purpose to see how I got on."

Then she darted to the doorway, whither John had modestly retreated, and pulled him in again.

"Herr Nicolai, this is the first master I ever had. He taught me when I was a tiny child."

Nicolai held out his hand, with that winning smile that made amends for all his short temper and severity, and shook John's warmly.

"I think we may be proud of our pupil," he said; "she does us credit."

"That she do, sir," said John; "yet far be it from me to take the credit unto myself. That child, sir, would have played, shut her up on a desert island; but proud I was to teach her what little I knew."

"Ah, and your band; how goes it? You see I am quite up in all you do at—how do you call it?—Keranstof? If you had more such bands in country places, you English would not be called the unmusical nation."

"Maybe so, sir; but when you say 'you English' you forget t'is different like in the Duchy, though haply t'is not as it was even there. Twenty year agoo ye wud'n have found many parishes in

Cornwall without their band; but now, what wi' their organs and their harmoniums and such like, the music is dyin' out fast. And we get so many more foreigners come amongst us than used to be."

Nicolai looked at Jenifer in some perplexity. "I don't quite understand," he said. "Cornwall is in England, isn't it?"

Jenifer laughed. "Oh yes; but you can rarely get a Cornishman to admit it. In fact, there is a difference of race as there is in Brittany; and we do flatter ourselves that we are more musical than the South of England, at any rate."

Then, leaving him and John to fight the matter out, she went back to Studland, who was standing beside Frau Klieschmann, inattentively answering the remarks with which she was trying to entertain him, while eye and ear were occupied with the little group on his other hand.

"I have not congratulated you yet, Captain Studland," she said.

"Thanks! On which?" he asked, looking round and pulling his brown beard.

"On both. On your promotion as well, of course; but I meant your engagement. I hope you will both be very happy." Inwardly she could not help remarking, "How changed he is! He never used to have any swagger."

"Thanks, very much."

He did not seem to have any more to add, and she went on—

"I wrote to Letty to give her my good wishes. You will not go on living at Pencoet, I suppose?"

"No; Pencoet will have to be given up this year. We shall be at Portsmouth; and I am looking out for a furnished house at Southsea. It will be rather a change for Letty, after such an ancient dwelling-place; but she will find plenty to amuse her. I hear you will be at Kerranstow at Easter."

"I hope so. This touring engagement will be over by the end of March, and then I want to get a few weeks at home before I begin in town."

"Then we shall hope to see you at our wedding. It is to be the second week in April. Has Letty sent you an invitation in due form?"

It is uphill work congratulating people who do not respond with any enthusiasm, and Jenifer was not sorry that at this moment Nicolai came up to her, and said, with an air of proprietorship—

"I am going to send your friends away, Miss Lyon, and make you rest a few minutes. Alfredi is just gone on, and you must keep quiet and collect yourself, or you will not do as well as you did just now."

He drew forward a chair and placed her with her back to the company, and remorselessly swept away her visitors.

Two or three songs had taken place unnoticed while they were behind the scenes, and at the end of the tenor solo she reappeared, fiddle in hand, to be greeted with a round of applause.

This time she played a Nocturne of Nicolai's

own composition; a tender, pensive thing, that showed her qualities in quite a different vein from the wild, reckless Scherzo. After a dreamy opening, the motive was wrought up into the agitation of passionate longing, to die down again into the same soft, tender refrain. Alick sat with his hand over his eyes, listening, not as a musician listens to progressions and modulations, but as though he heard her voice recalling to his memory a certain long-past Christmas Eve, when he and she sat side by side in a sheltered nook halfway down the Shag's Head. The chance had lain in his hand then. What had he done with it? and why? At the end he looked up to see her bowing her thanks as the people clapped, and like a cold douche he realized her remoteness. She was nothing to him, nor he to her; never could be now.

"Are you very tired, Alick?" said Septimus's voice in his ear. "I am afraid this sort of thing bores you. Do you care about stopping to the end?"

When all was over, they made their way round to the performers' room again to bid Jenifer good-bye, for Mr. Jaques had a funeral next day, and they must be early on the road. They found her being carefully wrapped up by Nicolai, and looking rather white and tired. She would not hear of parting with them so abruptly; she was just going to send and fetch them, she said, to go home and have supper with her and Frau Klieschmann. Herr Nicolai had promised to come, and it would be their only chance of hearing him play, and one they ought not to miss. Why, John must come too, of course; she would not have any of them unless John came.

She had her way, and they all repaired to the quiet little lodging that she and her chaperon preferred to the hotel and the company of the vocalists. It was a new view of little Jenifer to see her entertaining a party of gentlemen to an after-performance supper; for she was hostess, though the good Frau was excellent to play propriety. And very well she did it too, with a quiet simplicity and naturalness that took off any flavour of Bohemianism.

The meal over, and the gentlemen provided with cigarettes, Frau Klieschmann, whom long practice had rendered an excellent accompanist, went to the piano, and Nicolai began tuning a violin, the mere sound of which thrilled John Yeo to the marrow of his bones. Jenifer herself did not play; she had done her part at the concert, and leant back in an easy-chair by the fire, enjoying John's ecstasy, and only disturbed by the uneasy sense of Alick's eyes upon her; for in such a company the music precluded conversation.

But John, at least, was happy; he was rapt away from the world of work and everyday cares into a realm where music is all in all. And Nicolai played on to him and to his master with as much zest, as hearty an enjoyment of their pleasure, as he had ever felt in a crowded concert-room, till the striking of a clock suddenly warned them that they had trespassed half an hour beyond midnight.

They all took leave in a hurry then; but while Studland was struggling into his great-coat in the narrow passage the vicar came inside the room to put on his, and have a few last words with Jenifer.

"Is anything the matter with Captain Studland?" she asked him in a low voice, seeing the room empty but for Frau Klieschmann; "he does not seem himself to-night."

"He is certainly a little absent and distrait, but I suppose we must make allowance; he has probably left his heart at Pencoet."

She smiled. "I suppose that is it. I wondered whether they were having any bothers about settlements or things of that sort; they are often so troublesome. He seemed so unresponsive when I congratulated him."

"Oh, I believe not. The course of true love seems running very smooth this time. But Studland is an undemonstrative fellow — singularly undemonstrative. Well, good-bye. We shall see you down at Kerranstow in good time for the wedding?"

She turned back to the fire when they were gone, and stood looking into it till Frau Klieschmann came and put an arm affectionately round her waist.

"I congratulate you, dear, on your triumph—for it was a triumph to-night, having Nicolai there, and Mr. Jaques and all, and doing so splendidly.

I was so thankful you were not nervous. I am sure it was enough to make you so to see Herr Nicolai's exacting eyes devouring you from the front row, and then catching sight of your friends all at once. It was a mercy it did not overset you; but I never heard you play better."

She stopped and kissed her. Jenifer returned her embrace, and moved a little wearily to light her bedroom candle."

"You must be tired out, dear; you are very pensive."

"I suppose I am rather tired; it was hard work, and rather an exciting evening altogether. But I enjoyed it; oh yes, I enjoyed it."

But as she went upstairs she was saying to herself, "But he isn't happy; I know he isn't."

CHAPTER VI.

"GOING already, Alick? Why shouldn't you stay and dine? You need not be afraid of Mrs. Grundy, though Violet is not here, for Jenifer Lyon has promised to come and spend the evening with me; so, besides the attractions of my society, there is her music to tempt you. What do you say to that?"

And Letty, who was the speaker, laid a detaining hand on Studland's coat-sleeve.

"No, no, thanks," he answered a little shortly; "I can't possibly stop. Don't you know," he added, with a smile, "I have some very particular business to transact on the way back?"

"Business? No, what is it?"

"Why, don't you recollect what is to happen the day after to-morrow? I have to give in our banns for next Sunday. By the way, I had almost forgotten to ask you; have you a second name besides Letitia? We must have it all correct."

"Letitia indeed! You wretch! The idea of taking me for an embodied sneeze! How angry

I should have been if I had heard Mr. Jaques read me out in church as Letitia. I should certainly have jumped up and forbidden my own banns. No—Lettice Audrey; and mind you don't forget."

"All right; I won't forget. And now I really must be on my way."

Yet he lingered a minute, and looked at Letty wistfully as he wished her good night.

"My Letty," he said, more gravely than he often spoke to her; "I wish you were not quite such a little will-o'-the wisp. In less than three weeks you will be my wife, and yet, somehow, I never feel sure of you. Since we have been engaged, you seem to slip further and further out of my grasp." As he spoke he tried to draw her nearer to him.

"Nonsense," she said, disengaging herself from his arm; "you know I hate heroics; and I am not very fond of these kind of demonstrations."

"Neither am I particularly," he said; "yet—but, however, it is not a case for argument. No doubt you are right, and we shall shake down together by and by as well, or better, than if we indulged in moonshine now." And he turned to go.

"Now don't be tiresome. I didn't mean to be cross. Well, there then; will that content you?" and putting up her face, she deposited a butterfly kiss somewhere on the borders of his beard.

And with this unsatisfactory salute he was fain to depart. Satisfied he was not, and he hardly knew whether the want was in her or in himself.

He had turned his back resolutely, as a wise man should, on that glimpse of what might have been that had come upon him so unlooked for when he saw Jenifer in her matured beauty and womanliness, and had tried to solace himself with the charm and sweetness which in old days Letty had seemed to promise so abundantly; but he was conscious of a hunger for something she did not, perhaps could not, give him, and a feeling akin to poor Oliver's of being tied to an Elle-woman was growing on him.

She had gone out to the door with him, and when he disappeared, stood a few minutes watching a procession of little ragged clouds scudding across the face of the moon. It was a windy March evening, but not cold, and here in the doorway it was sheltered. She was alone for a few days; next week her sisters were coming down to help her in her preparations, but just now there was an interval of comparative leisure, and she had been able to see more of her betrothed than she had done since they had been engaged.

"I hope I did not vex him, poor old boy," she said to herself. "I am afraid he finds me cold— and I am cold. I suppose it is a peculiarity of mine. I can be very nice to people at first, but when they want more of me, I shrink up. I wonder if I should have been like that if I had married a man I loved when I was young? How odd it seems that next Tuesday fortnight I shall have left my old self behind me and started afresh.

I think we shall get on very well. As a rule, he is rather chary of caresses himself; only, I suppose, just now, with our wedding so near, he thought he ought to show a little ardour. I don't think he will be exacting; and then he will be away a good deal."

At this point her meditations were interrupted by the sound of a gate opening—the gate in the garden wall by the side of the house that led by a flagged path under the library windows to the front door. Only visitors came in that way; those who had business in the back premises followed the drive down to the stable-yard. She made a step forward, thinking it would be Jenifer.

It was not Jenifer, however, but a tall man, who was advancing along the white flags.

"Why, Alick," she cried; "have you forgotten something, or thought better——" and then broke off abruptly, for it was not Alick either. The visitor was wearing a heavy travelling ulster, with a great hood thrown back over his shoulder, and the confusing half-light contending with the moon just caught the outline of a cheek clear of beard, but crossed by a wide-spreading light moustache.

Letty stood still and awaited his coming. She could not well go in and shut the door in his face, whoever he might be, but her knees began to shake under her with a curious premonition.

"Is Mrs. Dendron——? Oh, I beg your pardon, I could not see. I need not ask if you are at home."

The soft, well-bred voice did not suggest a tramp or dangerous beggar, but Letty stood speechless, looking at him as if he had been a burglar or a ghost.

"I am afraid I startled you," he went on, with compunction in his tone. "I am awfully sorry. You have not forgotten me"—reproachfully—"Latimer?"

Letty rallied then. "Oh, Mr. Latimer!" she cried; "what a reception to give you. I beg your pardon; but I really thought for a moment you must be your own ghost. I had no idea you were in England. Do come in."

"Are you sure that you are, technically speaking, 'at home'? It is really disgraceful of me to call at such an unheard-of hour; but I was impatient. If you are busy, pray tell me; I can call just as well to-morrow."

"No, no," she cried; "you must come in, of course." She held out her hand. "Ah, I see you are really flesh and blood, and do not melt into thin air when I touch you, as I half expected," she added, with a nervous laugh.

He stepped into the hall, and as he divested himself of his overcoat, the lamplight showed a very handsome, distinguished-looking man of about forty, with intensely blue eyes, looking the bluer in contrast to a rather brown and sallow skin.

"How did you come, and when? And won't you have something after your journey?" asked

Letty, leading the way to the drawing-room, and fluttering nervously about.

"No, thanks. I don't want anything but to see you," he answered her last query. "I got something at a sort of halfway house on the crest of the moor. I come straight from town *viâ* Bridesworth. I really had no business to come frightening you at this time in the evening. I did intend settling myself at the inn first, and coming in due form to-morrow morning, but when I had got so near I found I could not wait. And, moreover, I lost my way in these wonderfully meandering lanes, and that made me a bit later than I should have been."

"Thank Heaven for that!" was Letty's mental ejaculation. "And yet, after all, it might have been better if he had arrived ten minutes earlier and found Alick here, for then he would have guessed how things are, and I should not have had to tell him."

She seated herself opposite to him with a feather screen in her hand, and began to talk volubly, pouring out a string of questions about Moscow and St. Petersburg, which he responded to absently, with his eyes on the fire, pulling his long moustache. Presently, when she paused to take breath, he roused up, and leaning forward, said suddenly—

"So you are a free woman now, Letty!"

The hand holding the screen dropped into her lap, and she sat gazing at him, without finding a word to say in answer.

He gave a little, soft laugh.

"Don't look so shocked, and forgive me if I have outraged your sense of what is due——" He glanced across at a sombre portrait of Oliver which rested on an easel behind her. "It is a full year surely, and seeing you wearing colours, I thought the past was past."

"It is very evident," said Letty, trying to speak lightly, though her mouth was dry, "that you cannot have seen any of my friends in town, or else that my affairs are not so interesting as I supposed they were. You cannot have heard that I am going to be married shortly."

He rose from his seat with a smothered exclamation, and for half a minute there was dead silence. Then Letty spoke.

"Aren't you going to congratulate me?"

"No. Did you suppose it likely I should? I imagine you know, or can guess, what brought me home."

She, too, had risen to her feet, and throwing off the artificial manner in which she had been speaking, locked her hands together, and said—

"Oh, Philip, why didn't you write?"

"And if I had?"

His eyes were fixed on her, forcing a reply. She averted hers.

"Don't!" she said. "It is too late."

"Write!" he went on. "Did you expect me to write and condole with you on your loss? When I saw the announcement in the paper it seemed to me the only thing I could do in common decency was to wait; and then I was sent off on a mission to the interior of Thibet. I have been there for months, cut off from letters, from news, from everything; and when I found myself once more in St. Petersburg, it seemed to me the best plan was to get six weeks' leave and come straight off. Don't imagine that I reproach you. I have nothing to say. I was mistaken; that is all."

She was leaning on the mantelpiece, with her face averted. He drew nearer.

"Well, good-bye," he said; "there is no use in my staying longer. Try and forget this episode, as I shall do. Why, you are crying! Oh, by Heaven, I can't leave you like this! Tell me, Letty, what it is you mean?"

"That I am miserable," she answered, without raising her head. "It is too late; you had better go."

"Miserable! Then why on earth are you doing it?"

"I don't know!" she sobbed. "I was very lonely, and I drifted into it. I never dreamt you thought of me still, or that I should ever see or hear of you again."

"You are not in love with him then, this fellow you are going to marry?"

"No. I like him; I am fond of him. I hate the thought of treating him badly. But in love —no."

"Do you love me?"

He tried to look into her eyes, but she would not raise her head.

"I don't know. I hate you sometimes. You have made me more wretched than any one else could ever do."

"Ah well; I would be very well satisfied with that kind of hatred. You and I belong to each other, and I don't mean to be baulked a second time. This other man shall give you up."

"Don't; you frighten me. You shall not make me break faith."

"Faith! I am not so sure about that. Some promises are better in the breach than in the observance. It seems to me you will keep truer faith by breaking with him than by vowing to do what you can't do. You may think that after to-night you will be able to feel just as you did before I came, while you imagined me at St. Petersburg. I tell you you won't do anything of the kind. I am not a dream or a ghost; and you won't forget me as easily as you fancy."

"Forget you! I only wish I could. Oh, why will you torture me so? I cannot, cannot do what you wish." Then, with a sudden change of tone, she added, "Why, my frocks are all made, and our banns are to be asked on Sunday."

"That can be put a stop to; and as to the frocks, they will do beautifully to take out. We have not much time to spare; I have to be at my post again the first week in May. Ah, Letty, it is the very life for you! I have often thought what a wife you would make for a foreign *attaché;* and I am going up fast. Would not your ambitious little ladyship like to see herself as Russian or Austrian Ambassadress, eh? And there is no telling where I may stop. When your mother frowned upon a penniless younger son she did not foresee what powerful connections and brains together might accomplish. I can put you in a position worthy of you."

Letty flashed round on him then.

"I will not be tempted with that sort of bait," she cried. "If you put it on that ground, I shall say no, no; a thousand times no. I cannot be so mean."

"Well, you were less squeamish when you threw me over for poor Dendron's money-bags."

"Remember how young I was, and what mother's determination is. And, besides, until it was all done, I don't think I realized how much you were to me. Then that unlucky quarrel; I declare at the time I thought it was you that were throwing me over; and then nothing seemed to matter. Certainly I never dreamed you were the sort of man who would have remained true to me after the way I treated you. I was always expecting to hear that you were married."

"Well, I am not going to pretend that I have never looked at another woman since we parted, and I don't suppose you would believe me if I did; but I can truly say I never yet met the woman for whose sake I would barter my freedom except you. I have seen handsomer women, but never another whose beauty did not pall upon me."

He watched the effect of his words, and he could see that Letty was wavering.

"And you really don't think me gone off?" she asked, in more of her natural manner than she had yet spoken.

"Rubbish!" he laughed. "As if you did not know that you are prettier than ever."

He knew his cause was won then, but he made a feint of going.

"Now, Letty," he said, "I must go; and the time has come for a decision. You must choose for yourself. If you send me away without an answer to-night, you will never see me again."

She stood before him, not facing him, but looking down at the hearthrug at her feet.

"What you ask is impossible. It is too late. I could not do it."

He took a few steps towards the door.

"No, no. Oh, Philip, what do I care! I cannot let you go."

He turned and held out his arms without speaking, and she flung herself into them.

Meanwhile Jenifer had arrived, driven in the jingle by Thomas the "boy," and since in that unprotected conveyance it was necessary to be well wrapped up, she had betaken herself to Letty's room to take off her things. The maid who engagement had been. It was some days, however, before anything transpired about Philip Latimer. He disappeared on Sunday night from Kerranstow, and on Monday morning, instead of the arrival of the expected sisters, Letty and her trousseau in many large trunks took the early coach to go up to her mother's house in London. She could not face Kerranstow and produce Philip Latimer there; she was too deeply ashamed of the part she had played. The old house was shut up, and soon bills of "To Let" were displayed looking over the garden wall, and Pencoet would know her no more.

Septimus was even more shocked and distressed than the chief sufferer. He gave Alick credit for having his heart more deeply involved than was really the case, and Letty's treachery seemed to revive afresh the memory of his own old painful story. If there had been no real attachment to Alick, her former conduct was more utterly inexcusable; and his wrath blazed up more hotly against her as he recalled how she had beguiled his judgment to lenience on that occasion. In his lonely life the freshness and keenness of his sympathies had been preserved as they seldom are beyond middle age. Most men have expended their stock of feeling on wife and children by the time they are fifty; it is often the solitary who have most pity to spare. He had always had a warm corner in his heart for Alick, whom he had watched grow up from boyhood, and who had often come to him in his young days for the comfort and counsel he could not always get from the parents and home that were not really his. So if Mrs. Dendron had not seen fit to take herself off, it is extremely probable she would have received curt notice to quit. He was quite capable of refusing to allow roof of his to shelter any one of whose conduct he so utterly disapproved.

It may be imagined how the news was discussed at Roscorla. Louisa Twisselton positively gloated over it, and entertained herself and her mother by the hour in descanting on Letty's iniquities, and imagining all sorts of possible and impossible theories to account for the sudden breach. Poor Jenifer, who knew too much to be able to join in with any comfort in the discussion, was thankful when the weeping rain which had ushered in the first days of April was blown aside, and she was able to escape from the continual talk, and revisit some of her own well-loved haunts upon the cliffs.

Early spring is nowhere sweeter than on this north-west coast; the east wind which is the discouragement and scourge of our English spring in most parts, is a rare visitor here, and after the frequent showers that come like a sudden burst of tears, the fresh westerly breezes come sweeping across from the sea and bringing the sunshine back again. The wet granite shines and sparkles like a smile on an old man's face. In the shelter of the hollow ways, the deep-cut lanes that connect one lone farm with another, the shy primroses and the little blue stars of the periwinkle are peeping out, and will soon eclipse the pert celandines which have of late arrogated the whole hedgerow to themselves. Down at the bottom of the deep combes, underneath the brushwood, the windflowers droop their meek heads, and the breezy upland will soon be like cloth of gold with the gorse.

Jenifer took her way down the combe from Roscorla and over the heights of Corbie crag, as heedless of wet boots and of the effect on her skirts of the narrow prickly rabbit tracks between the furze as in her old days; and loaded with spoil—primroses and windflowers and some great boughs of blackthorn that looked as if laden with fresh-fallen snow—she reached the path down to her favourite nook on the Shag's Head. Her booty she deposited in a sheltered cranny near the top where the wind would not blow it away; she knew she should want both hands for the descent.

The rough storms of last winter had rather damaged the path; in places it was quite crumbled away, and she needed a watchful eye on her footsteps as she let herself carefully down from one ledge to another. Thus it came about that until she reached the platform which was her goal, she did not perceive that it was already occupied. Alick Studland was sitting on a rock looking out to sea. As she jumped down the last few feet he looked round and saw her, hastening to offer his help just too late.

Retreat was impossible now, though she felt annoyed with herself that she had not seen him in time to turn back unobserved; so she came forward with a remark about the pleasantness of finding all her old nooks unaltered.

People often complain that it is a difficult and trying task to condole with friends in affliction; it is far worse to meet with one's friends under some stroke that must be ignored, in which compassion would be an impertinence and cheerfulness seems heartless. It was not easy to meet naturally; still less so in that precise spot which recalled to both how they had once sat there together and talked of Letty; though by a curious irony of fate it had been he who had warned Jenifer against her fascinations upon that occasion.

If they had encountered each other in any ordinary way, to exchange a word or two and pass on would have been easy enough; but for either abruptly to leave this place, so difficult of access, would seem like a deliberate attempt to avoid each other. Jenifer wished she had Letty's gift for getting over hard places by a trivial flow of conversation; she did her best, but her efforts were suddenly scattered to the winds by a question from Alick.

"Have you heard from Mrs. Dendron since she went away?"

"Once. You know she is gone to her mother's.

Nothing was fixed when she wrote, but I imagine she will marry very soon and go out to St. Petersburg."

"Thanks. I wanted to know, and it is little likely she and I will ever hold any communication again."

Then he smiled a little at the startled look Jenifer had not been able to banish from her face at his question, and added—

"You think it odd my mentioning her. I suppose it is, but I am going away almost immediately, and before I went I thought it would be a satisfaction to know what had become of her. I might have asked Mr. Jaques to find out for me; but his indignation is so hot against her, I dare not mention the subject to him. I am not vindictive; I should like to know that she had got what she wanted."

Jenifer was puzzled. Was this the stoical indifference of a man who would not betray a mortal wound? She could not tell. She hardly knew what to say.

"That sounds very generous," she began.

"And cold-blooded. But you know, Miss Lyon, I cannot help feeling I have had an escape. Every man likes to feel he has a wife he can trust; but for a sailor anything else is destruction. Of coure I was furious at first—who would not have been? No man relishes being made a fool of; but I have come to see that things being as they were, she did the best she could in speaking out."

It was an immense relief to hear him say so, and Jenifer's face showed it.

"I am glad you think that," she said.

"Ah," he said, "was it your advice that gave her the pluck to speak instead of cutting the knot in some easier and less creditable fashion?"

Her eyes fell, and her face flamed.

"I tried not to advise her. She would tell me about it because I happened to be there that night he came; for a long while I would not say what I thought; but when she pressed me I did say that I believed truth was the safest plan. Did I do wrong? I have been so afraid you might think so. People feel so differently on such a matter."

"You did right and wisely, and I thank you for it; don't torment yourself with fancying I should have wished her differently advised. And don't pity me too much," he added, seeing the look of distress on her face. "Even if I had been very hard hit, I don't think I could digest compassion; as it is, I would rather that those who have known all about it should understand that though it has been very painful and odious, it was in truth a somewhat superficial matter on both sides. Must you be going back? Let me go first then, and give you a hand."

As they climbed up the steep pathway, he a little in advance, he went on—

"One of the most trying parts of the whole business has been the being watched with so much solicitude to see how I took it. I suppose it is really an evidence of kindly feeling, but it is uncommonly disagreeable. It would have been much the same if I had gone back to Portsmouth at once; of course all my shipmates knew what I had leave for, and when I go back wifeless I shall have to run the gauntlet of much sympathy; so I thought I might just as well brazen it out here for a week or so, and let the good folks see that I was not killed."

At the top they parted. His hand closed round hers with a warm clasp.

"I am glad I met you. It has been comfortable to talk it out with some one that understood."

CHAPTER VIII.

STUDLAND was growing rather morose. His friends of course said that he was a good deal more cut up about Mrs. Dendron's—now Mrs. Latimer's—conduct than he suffered to appear at first. The annoyance of the affair had certainly been considerable, and the minor disagreeables had come into all the greater prominence since there was no broken heart in the case to swallow up all lesser evils. Yet it was not altogether that.

Of late he had taken a great interest in music; he took in several musical reviews, and studied the accounts of concerts with great attention. A hunger was coming over him to hear Jenifer play again; but for some time he refrained from rushing up to town to gratify it, for he had an instinctive feeling that he had better hold himself back awhile; Jenifer would not be likely to care for a heart caught in the rebound. Indeed, judging from the way she had eluded him for years past, he feared she would be little likely to care for him at all.

The season went by, and she was in Cornwall again for rest; but he had had his share of leave in winter and spring, and must bide his time. At last, towards the end of the autumn, he saw an announcement that Miss Lyon had been engaged to play at a series of concerts to be given every Saturday at Bournemouth, and he resolved he would indulge himself with a sight of her. He went over by boat, and as he walked up the pier speculated which hotel was likely to contain her. It would be a great piece of good fortune if he could meet with her beforehand. Judging from his experience of her tastes, he fancied the probabilities were in favour of the one nearest the sea, so thither he decided to betake himself.

He ordered an early dinner, so as to be in plenty of time, and while it was being brought, amused himself by studying the entries in the visitor's book, but without finding the name he sought. But as he turned the pages listlessly, another name caught his eye, and he uttered an exclamation, "Denis Kay, Melbury Road, Kensington." Was this man really going to forestall and baulk him yet once more? He threw down the book.

The waiter caught the exclamation just as he was setting down the dish that Studland had ordered, and glanced at the open page.

"Do you know that gentleman, sir? Mr. Kay, the painter? He is very ill, I am afraid, sir. He came down yesterday, and was took very bad with the influenza. Perhaps, if you are a friend of his, you would like to see him, sir? That is if you are not afraid of the infection; some do say it is catching."

"Ill, is he? I am very sorry. Yes, I do know him. When I have dined, you can take up my card, and ask if he would care to see me. Say I should be very glad if I could be of any use to him."

"Thank you, sir, I will. 'Tis very lonesome for the poor gentleman to lie there by himself all day, and that influenza is a nasty complaint."

Presently the waiter returned. Mr. Kay was much obliged, and would be very glad to see him. So he was conducted upstairs and down a long passage, and ushered into a room where Denis, looking very small and very forlorn, lay in the middle of an enormous four-post bed. Beside him on a chair stood an untouched cup of broth and a cup of tea half full, both stone-cold of course.

"This is really awfully kind of you," he said, leaning forward and trying to clear the chair of its encumbrance for his visitor.

"No, don't trouble. Here," to the waiter, "take these things away, and bring up a small cup of beef-tea, will you? Nonsense"—as Denis made a gesture of refusal—"the one thing I know about influenza is that you ought to go on drinking beef-tea *ad lib*. We had the whole ship down with it at one time, and I well remember how they kept pouring the stuff down my throat."

Evidently Studland had no idea of sitting down

and being entertained as a visitor, and the sick man watched him with content as he moved softly about the room with a step as light as a woman's, and the true sailor knack of making the best of whatever came to hand, arranging things comfortably, mending the fire, and shading the patient's eyes from the light. Failing that rare specimen of her sex who is truly "a born nurse," there is no better to be found than a sailor; I suppose because they have learned not to depend on the ministrations of womankind.

Kay, however, felt bound to protest. "Oh, please don't trouble; there is no occasion really; the nurse will be here presently; she'll do all that."

"Will she? Don't you make too sure. At any rate she shall find all things ship-shape."

Presently the beef-tea made its tardy appearance, and after the patient had swallowed it unresistingly he seemed drowsy and disinclined to talk; yet Studland could not make up his mind to leave him all alone. To his eye he appeared seriously ill; and it was dreary for the poor fellow to be left to the chance ministrations of a good-natured, but harassed and over-driven waiter. At any rate he thought he would stay till the doctor came, as he understood he had promised to do before evening, to introduce the nurse.

The time was slipping by. If he was going to that concert he ought to be dressing. Eight o'clock struck. Well, he had missed the first thing, anyway, which Jenifer was to play. He took out his programme and studied it, trying to see her in his mind's eye as he had seen her at that concert at Exeter last spring. Denis woke, looking more feverish than ever, and wanted something to drink. That he took Alick's presence for granted and made no remark was in itself a bad sign. By this time the latter realized that there was no concert for him that evening; if he was to hear Jenifer play, it must be on some future Saturday.

He had himself dozed off in his chair when the doctor made his appearance, with a fagged and harassed air, and an open telegram in his hand.

"Oh!" he said, as his eye fell on Studland, "I am glad he has some one with him; he ought not to be left at night; and, look here, I have just had this"—holding out the slip of paper. It was from the nurse who had been sent for, to say that it was out of the question for her to come that night; she hoped to be able to get down by the first train on Sunday morning.

"And there is not a single nurse I know of disengaged in the place. I never knew such a sickly season."

The doctor's coming roused Kay to insist that Alick should go; there was not the least occasion for any one to sit up with him; he should do very well if they would put a glass of water by his bed, he was rather thirsty.

"I shall stay, of course," said Studland, following

the doctor into the passage. "What do you think of him?"

"Well, he certainly is not better. There is considerable fever; but I don't suppose we could reasonably expect any improvement yet. Mind he takes something every two hours at the least, and keep a good fire in; that is really the chief thing."

Alick returned to the room, finding he had practically no choice but to remain, and very willing, in this way, to put coals of fire on his enemy's head—supposing that Denis was his enemy.

"I wonder," he said to himself, as he made up the fire, and settled himself in an armchair beside it, "why on earth he has not married her all these years. What does the fellow mean by dangling after her? He had no right to do it—spoiling her life."

He took a book for awhile, but he was no great reader, and he soon let it fall from his hand; his own thoughts were more interesting; they were occupied with Jenifer and his love for her. Finding Denis Kay here had thrown his mind back to those early days when he had come home from the West Indies to find, as he thought, his "little wife," as he used to call her in his own fancy, and the painter had come between. He knew very well if he had felt for her then a tithe of what he felt now, he would not have been so easily set aside; and she had not been engaged to Kay after all. He might have won her then; and now here was

Kay once more, and this time it was probably too late. He had allowed himself to be convinced on the testimony of the pearl necklace; he had set his love aside as a foolish, baseless fancy; he had let it be stifled under another and very different kind of love, and, instead of dying under the treatment, a new love had arisen from the ashes, and was avenging itself on him.

Something strange and new, that he had not known it was in him to feel, had come to him suddenly when he saw her before him on the platform that night at Exeter; something which, end as it might, made him devoutly thankful to Letty for her infidelity. His was not a sanguine temper at any time, and when he recalled how much Jenifer had known of his past history, and the quiet way in which she had spoken of Letty when he last saw her at Kerranstow, he could not flatter himself with any hopes.

There was a little movement from the bed, and he turned to see how his patient was getting on. He was not asleep, but lay, with wide eyes, watching him.

"Can I get you anything?"

"No; I only wanted to say how awfully sorry I am I let you stay. I was in such a fog this evening I never thought of anything; but I have just recollected about the concert. I suppose I am right in fancying the same thing brought you down here that did me?"

"Ah!" said Studland, more resentfully than

he knew, "then you did come to hear her play?"

The other smiled. "Well, a cat may look at a king, I suppose?" he said quaintly. "It is always a great pleasure to me, and one that I never miss if I have the chance of it. I am glad to say she and I have always remained very good friends; though, as I dare say you may have guessed, I once hoped to have been something more."

Alick laid down the poker, and came to the foot of the bed.

"So that was it," he said. "Do you know, years ago, I was told that you were engaged to her, and I saw her wearing a necklace which I understood you had given her."

"Ah, that little necklace! she wears it yet; but it was not a love-token—it least, it was never accepted as one. I gave it her simply as a souvenir of the sittings she gave me for my picture; but I might have known what idle tongues would make of it. I am sorry; I feel as if I had taken an unfair advantage of her—she was such a child then; but perhaps you can understand the desire I felt to see it round her neck. I don't know exactly what made me mention the subject, except that it struck me that perhaps it concerned you to know the rights of it, and I learned from Mr. Jaques that there had been a false impression about it."

"It might have concerned me years ago; now—I don't know; I fancy it is too late."

"Oh, you fool!" said Denis.

"What do you mean?"

"Well, now, look here, before I tell you that, will you answer me a question? Do you care for her?"

Studland looked at him amazed for a moment, then answered gravely—

"With all my soul I do."

"Very well. Once, not so very long ago, I inadvertently said something to her that made her imagine for a moment that you were dead. She never said a word; but her face was enough. I wanted her to marry me then, but it stopped me; for I thought I saw what stood between. If you are in earnest, there is your encouragement."

"Thank you for telling me. This is a most extraordinary piece of generosity."

"No it is not, nothing of the kind. I did not want to over-persuade a woman to have me, while I imagined she cared more for some other fellow—not that I think I could, mind you; she is not the girl to belie her own feelings; but I could not even wish that she should. Of course you may have fooled away your chance by this time; I cannot tell how that may be; but she is not a changeable woman. Only one thing I will ask you; if she refuses you, will you let me know?"

"Certainly I will. I promise you that. I cannot help saying again that you are marvellously generous. I am afraid I should not have been capable of it. Feeling what I feel for her, the conducted her upstairs had rather a *tendresse* for the youthful Jehu, so she left her to disrobe herself while she slipped down the back stairs in order to waylay him with the seductive offer of a glass of mulled ale.

Jenifer wondered a little that Letty had not come out to greet her, but was sufficiently at home to find her own way downstairs without scruple. The door of the panelled parlour was not latched, and with a gentle push, it and the heavy *portière* that concealed it swung back without noise. She took a step forward, and then drew hastily back, seeing two figures standing locked in each other's arms upon the hearthrug. She had thought it possible that she might meet Alick Studland, but she had not bargained to make a third at such very unrestrained love-making. She could not help smiling to herself as she recalled a remark of Letty's, scoffing at such demonstrations, and declaring she always meant to make Alick keep his distance. This did not look much like it. Her two hands were clasped together behind his neck, and his head was bent down over hers, which was completely hidden against his breast.

As Jenifer stepped quickly back she raised her eyes for an instant, and caught a reflection in the mirror over the fireplace that almost forced an exclamation from her. It was not Alick. She distinctly saw a blonde head, slightly bald, and a long, fair moustache, resting on the top of Letty's hair. With an effort she kept herself from making the least sound, and flew upstairs again to the bedroom, panting with bewilderment and dismay.

What could it mean? Who could it be? Letty had no near relations that Jenifer had ever heard of; and besides, one does not greet father or brother even with such a passionate embrace. Only lovers could look as these two looked. And Letty was going to be married to another man within three weeks.

Poor, poor Alick! Was a suspicion of Letty's faithlessness making him so absent and unhappy when he came to hear her play at Exeter? Yet she did not believe it could have been so. He was not the man to sit tamely down under any such idea; to suffer himself to be hoodwinked, and go on with his engagement, if he thought he had any cause for uneasiness. No, he must be completely in the dark.

What a horrible position to be placed in. What could she do? Betray Letty? Never! Let Alick walk blindly into this snare? She must. Come what would, hers should never be the hand to interpose between him and the woman he had chosen.

She had only a minute or two before Letty came in, her eyes shining, her usually colourless cheeks glowing with the clear pink of strong excitement.

"My dear Jenifer"—kissing her—"have you been here long? I am afraid I am dreadfully late; I am so sorry."

"Not long; only a few minutes. There is something wrong with the bow of my shoe," said poor Jenifer, bending her head over it as though she were the culprit. "Can you give me a needle and thread?"

"I have no time to dress," went on Letty, flying round and pulling open drawers aimlessly; "but luckily I have got my favourite tea-gown on, so it won't matter. I have a friend dining here to-night—a very old friend, who I thought was away in the East. He came in just as I ought to have been going up to dress for dinner, and took me so by surprise. I am so glad you are here to help me to entertain him."

"Hardly necessary that," thought Jenifer, appearing to be absorbed in pushing her needle through the resisting kid of her shoe.

"Will you run down and make friends with him while I finish, or would you rather wait for me to introduce you in due form?"

"Oh, I will wait, thanks."

She was far from eager to make the acquaintance of the man downstairs; and, indeed, would fain have fled home upon her feet then and there, had such a course been feasible. Together they descended presently, Letty looking so lovely with that flush upon her face that there was no need of evening garb to heighten her beauty.

Jenifer felt as if she were performing her part in a stage play rather than in real life when she found herself presently sitting next the stranger, and responding pleasantly to his efforts to entertain her with most interesting accounts of life in Kashmir, where he had spent some time; of a secret mission to Thibet about a frontier question on which he had been sent; and anon reverting to the winter gaieties in St. Petersburg, where he had a post in the Embassy. The training in self-command which the habit of playing in public had given her stood her in good stead, and as Letty ably seconded her guest's conversation, the dinner passed off wonderfully. Had it not been for the extraordinary circumstances under which Jenifer had first seen him, she must have been fascinated by his gracefulness and perfect breeding.

She had come purposely to discuss final arrangements for the wedding; but, naturally, that subject was entirely tabooed. She wondered whether Letty observed her avoidance of it, and to what she would attribute it. The effort to keep the ball rolling as if there were nothing behind was not long protracted. About nine o'clock Mr. Latimer took his leave, saying to Letty, in a meaning tone, as he parted with her—

"I shall not see you to-morrow, probably; I think of going to Westcreek. May I call on Sunday?"

The two women were left together, and a silence fell upon them. Jenifer could not go, for the jingle was not ordered till ten. To escape from the oppression of an unspoken consciousness, she proposed that they should have some music. Letty gladly acceded, and opened the piano; but the thoughts of both were wandering. Jenifer had never played so ill, and the accompanist repeatedly lost her place. Presently she crashed down upon a chord, and broke off.

"It is no good, Jenifer; I cannot do a thing. To tell you the truth, I have something on my mind."

Jenifer stood looking at her, leaning on the end of the grand piano, her violin still in her hand. Letty turned a little on the music-stool, resting her elbows on the ledge, her chin on her hands.

"I have a need of confession," she said. "If Violet were here I should tell her. I think I shall make you my confessor."

An instinctive desire to say "Don't. You must decide for yourself; I cannot interfere," struggled with a sense that, knowing what she knew, she ought to listen to what Letty had to say for herself. She kept silence.

"A dreadful thing has happened to me, and I am at my wit's end. That man who was here just now—he was the first man, the only man, I ever cared for. Years ago, before I married, he and I were engaged—at least, that is to say, it was not a regular engagement, because we neither of us had any money, and our friends would not hear of it. They made mischief between us, and separated us; and then it did not seem to matter what I did—if you can't be happy, you may as well be rich—and I married poor Oliver. I had never heard from Philip since. He wouldn't write to me; he wouldn't even speak to me once when I met him in town. Of course, I thought he had forgotten me. He is the kind of man you would think would console himself easily; women always run after him, and he pretends to be so indifferent. And now, only think, he has come from Russia on purpose to ask me to marry him."

"I think you have treated Alick Studland abominably," was the only sentence which Jenifer could bring herself to utter.

"I know I have; I know it as well as you do. I am willing to cry *peccavi;* but the question is, not what I have done, but what I am to do."

"Don't ask me," cried Jenifer, with a gesture of despair. "How could I possibly advise you in such a crisis? How could any one?"

"Well, but you are a dispassionate observer," Letty went on; "and a person with a conscience, moreover. I know very well what I want to do; but I want to know whether, according to your code of right and wrong, the other course would be the right one. Is it my duty to trample on my own feelings, to tell Philip I will never see him again, to say nothing to any living soul of what has happened, and to carry out my engagement with all the happiness eaten out of my lot by the thought of what might have been? If you think that will make things right, and make Alick happy, say so. I don't say that I can do it; but I will at least consider it."

Jenifer laid down her violin and came forward.

"I will try and tell you what I think," she said. "If this had happened a month hence, you must have acted as you say; but, after all, a promise, though it is solemn, is not like a Sacrament. And there are promises that ought not to be kept in silence when there is something the other party to it ought to know. It is for Captain Studland to decide whether yours is to be kept or not. One thing I am certain of: you have no right to let him suppose you love him when you don't."

Letty looked at her for a minute without speaking. Jenifer was as white as a sheet, and when she ceased she sank into a chair.

"You had no right to lay such a cruel responsibility on me," she said; "but I cannot talk of it any more. After all, you must make your own decision. Whatever it is, you may rely on my absolute silence."

"Yes, I know I can trust you, Jenifer; you are as true as steel. Don't take it to heart so much. Why, it has made you look quite ill."

As they parted, Jenifer kissed her gravely, and said—

"I am very sorry for you, Letty; I am, indeed. I am afraid I seemed hard. I don't mean to be."

She went away; and Letty, whose mind was practically made up, had to decide on the further question: Should she see Alick, or should she write?

CHAPTER VII.

LETTY spent half the night in writing long exculpatory letters to her betrothed, and tearing them up before they were finished. Her waste-paper basket was filled to overflowing with the *débris*, but the only result of so much labour was a brief note which was put into his hand next morning, just as he was starting off for a neighbouring farm, in company with Rachel's little rough terrier, to join in a rat hunt. The young farmer who had come over to invite him to take part in this interesting function was with him, so he pocketed the missive without much thought, to open presently at some convenient opportunity. These little notes of hers were tolerably frequent; he got one every day or two to ask him to come to lunch, as she had business letters she wanted to consult him about; or not to come, as she was expecting the dressmaker. It would probably keep very well.

It must be owned he was rather enjoying these last days of his bachelor freedom. To be married to Letty would be very charming, but he would never be his own man again in quite the same way. He was conscious of a zest in the fresh free air of the moors, the keener in contrast to the warm, scented atmosphere of the panelled parlour. Two years ago, languid and depressed, he had fancied nothing could be sweeter than philandering about Pencoet, but now with restored vigour and energy, he had the feeling of being immeshed in silken fetters, and all the more disposed to appreciate a bit of barbaric sport.

It was not till the hunt was over, the terriers covered with glory, and gloating over heaps of slain, that, putting his hand into his pocket for his pipe, he encountered the stiff edge of Letty's epistle, and recollected with shame that he had never read it. It was short enough, but there was a tone of unusual urgency about the request—"Come and see me as early as you can. I have a special reason for wanting to see you without delay." Something must surely be the matter! He returned his pipe to his pocket, and declining a pressing invitation to lunch at the farm, though it was past two, and the exertions of the morning had given him a healthy appetite, he hurried to Pencoet.

As he set down his gun in the porch it struck him as strange that Letty did not come out to meet him as her custom was, especially if she was in such urgent haste for his coming; she must surely have heard him. He opened the door of the panelled parlour and went in. She was sitting by the fire, unoccupied, with a look of strained and anxious expectancy on her face; she rose and greeted him as though he were a stranger. He not unnaturally supposed her offended at his tardiness, and began to make excuse; but she cut him short.

"It does not matter. It is true I have been expecting you all the morning; but now you are come I am not ready for you."

"What is it?" he said, coming nearer. "There is something the matter. How strangely you look at me. My dear, are you ill?"

She signed him off with her hand.

"Oh, don't stand over me," she cried, irritably. "Do go and sit down upon the other side. I wish now I had written; at the time it seemed harder than to speak."

He looked at her, full of compassion; she was as white as a sheet and terribly agitated, as he could see from the way she was twisting her handkerchief into a rope; but he could not tell how to help her.

"My poor little darling," he said, "what can you be tormenting yourself about? Do try and tell me. You are making me horribly anxious. What in the world can have happened to you since I left you so bright and cheerful last night?"

She was almost angry with him for speaking so gently. If he had been cold and curt in manner, as of late he occasionally was, her task would have been easier; but to strike while he spoke in that tender, pitying way seemed brutal. She shrank; yet she knew it was no use to hesitate; if she turned aside and lost this chance, it would be still to do. She felt wrathful against Jenifer for her advice. "If it had not been for what she said," she thought to herself, "I believe I should have slunk away with Philip, leaving a letter behind me, and it would have been far better for us both than this horrible scene." However, she had made her choice, and she must go on. She nerved herself once more.

"I want, at this eleventh hour," she said, speaking in a dry, toneless voice, "to acknowledge to you that I have made a hideous, fatal mistake —to ask you to set me free."

In spite of her prohibition of "standing over her," he crossed the rug, and tried to take her hand.

"My dear Letty," he said, "this is a mere morbid fancy—a chimera. How could you possibly have made such an appalling discovery since I was here last night? You have been all alone, and have been brooding over what I said. I wonder at you. I always thought you such a practical little person. It just shows it is quite time you had somebody to take care of you."

"I am quite serious and in deadly earnest; it is no use your trying to turn it aside. How shall I make you see? I was not alone; after you left, I had a visit from a man I used to know—and loved, and nearly married years ago. Now do you understand?"

He had withdrawn to the station pointed out to him on the other side of the hearth, but remained standing.

"I think I do," he said in an altered tone. "It seems that you, plighted to me, suffered this old lover to propose to you again in ignorance of your position."

"I suppose it does—if you choose to put it in that brutal way."

"I hardly see how else to put it."

There was a minute's pause; she was fumbling with her engagement ring.

"Well?" she said at last, with breathless anxiety.

"Well? Oh, I see you are waiting for my answer. To me it seemed needless to say that I do not wish to marry a woman who prefers another man."

He held out his hand, and she dropped the ring into it.

"Alick," she cried, "it isn't fair; you force me to make the worst of myself—to put my conduct in the very blackest light. I know I have treated you badly; but I did not know what I was doing. I thought all that old business was over for ever. He has been abroad ever since I married. How could I tell he thought of me still?"

"And you accepted me as a *pis-aller*—a stop-gap

—till you should see whether your old lover would come forward again. Thank you. It is not a position I care to fill."

Although she wanted to be free, it was bitter to her praise-loving nature to be thus tossed aside; she felt as if it were he, not she, who was breaking off the engagement. She wanted to be relinquished, but with regret, and Alick's manner stung her. The penitent tears she had been on the brink of shedding, dried up, and when he spoke again, her composure was equal to his.

"I suppose there is no more to be said." He stooped to pick up his hat. "And I have no wish to linger. Your letters shall be returned to-night."

His eye fell on Oliver's portrait in its conspicuous position, as Philip Latimer's had done last night.

"There seems to be a kind of poetical justice in it,"—he laughed grimly—"I fear you and I went to the verge of indiscretion once, and did not act quite fairly by him; but he is avenged, and it is my turn now. Only I am so much the more fortunate that you have changed your mind now rather than later, and for that I thank you. Good-bye."

His hand touched hers for a second, and that story was finished.

Next morning an unusually good congregation filled Kerranstow Church. Banns always acted as a draw; but the banns of such an important personage as the tenant of Pencoet, to say nothing of its being the consummation of a so much discussed engagement, possessed an attraction positively dramatic.

The Second Lesson was concluded, and in a hush of expectancy every eye was turned to Mr. Jaques as he re-entered the reading-desk. John Yeo, who to-day was filling the combined offices of clerk and verger, and had therefore relinquished the leadership of the band to Abel Polsue, looked up at the musician's gallery, and signed emphatically that they should proceed. But Abel was a slow thinker and tenacious of an idea once received; it had been intimated to him on Saturday that the banns of Alick Studland, bachelor, of the parish of Hennacombe, and Lettice Audrey Dendron, widow, of this parish, were to be read, and until that was accomplished he would wait with suspended bow, if he waited till his dying day. It was perfectly useless for John to wink and signal, so at last, perceiving the futility of his efforts, he stood up in his desk and putting his hand to his mouth, said in a stentorian whisper—

"Goo on, wull 'ee; 'tis 'O be joyful.'"

But Abel, almost doubling his body over the front of the gallery, till the occupants of the pew beneath fully expected to have him in their laps, whispered hissingly back—

"Pa'son have forgot the banns."

But at that instant, just in time to prevent recriminations or awkward explanations, Septimus's powerful voice was heard, not in the banns, but in the opening words of the *Jubilate*. The congregation rose to their feet, looking at each other in a bewildered way, and the band, roused at length to a sense of their duty, hurried after him, only overtaking him as he reached the *Gloria*.

"Whativer can hev' made pa'son forget them banns?" said Peninah to Grace Yeo, almost before they were outside the church door. "I wonder your goodman didn't put him in mind, same as Abel Polsue was a-tryin' to. Do 'ee suppose he'll rade un this evenin'?"

"I d'knaw," responded Grace. "'Tis a quare job, seemin'ly. John ain't said nawthin' to me about it; but I should judge it must have been put off likely. I see they weren't nayther one on 'em there."

"Oh, as to that," said the astute Peninah, "the quality is always bashful like about hearin' theirselves out-asked in church. Besides, maybe he is lookin' to it that old Mr. Treby don't make no mistake up to Hennacombe."

The choir and band were coming out now, clattering down the little winding stair, and John, who had just issued from the vestry, received Abel Polsue with reproaches.

"You Abel Polsue, you'm not fit to be the leader of this here band, if you'm such a thickheaded donkey as not to goo on playin' when I signs to ye."

"Well," remonstrated Abel, in an injured tone,

"there was banns to be asked, and they hadn't a'ben asked, and if I had a went on playin' 'twould ha' ben—'Why was you such a ass as not to leave time for them banns when you knawed as they was a-gooin' to be asked?'"

"And who told you as they was a-gooin' to be asked? 'Tis for pa'son and me to decide whether us'll rade them or whether us won't rade them, and if us chooses to leave them out 'tisn't for such as you to interfere."

"Ah should think the bridegroom'd be like to interfere when a knaws a ain't been out-asked in this parish. T'weddin' will hev' to be put off."

"You can leave we to settle with the bridegroom. How do you knaw they don't mean to be married by licence, after all?"

And with this ingenious suggestion, Yeo went his way. That morning, going up to the church, his master had said to him—"Mrs. Dendron's banns are postponed, but I don't wish anything said about it." So village gossip should get nothing from him.

Mr. Jaques himself was almost in the dark. On the Saturday evening a brief note had been left at the Vicarage while he was at church—"Cancel the banns. We part by mutual consent." And until he heard more he would utter no word on the subject.

In spite of his and John's discretion, however, before nightfall the news was public property, and was a nine days' wonder no less than the thought of standing back and giving a chance to another man—— No, I could never have done it."

"Perhaps I couldn't a few days ago; I don't know. I seem to have been lying here for centuries, looking on at life as if I were a spectator. Why should I be a dog in the manger? And I know that what I want is hopelessly out of reach. If I could make her marry me, unless she loved me, I wouldn't do it."

They were both silent for a little while; then Studland said—

"After all you may have been mistaken. I cannot buoy myself up with hope. If she were a stranger I might; but when I recollect how long I have known her, and how every year she has grown colder and more aloof from me, I despair."

"That is no reason; she was always very kind to me. There have been times when her quiet friendliness has cut me to the quick. Don't you suppose that the more she cared for you, the less she was likely to show it? Such women as she are little apt to betray a preference for a man who shows them none."

"True. How I have been befooled. I drew back thinking her fickle. And all the time—oh, Heaven, what I may have missed!"

"How talking of her brings back the old Kerranstow days," went on Kay—"the first evening I ever saw her, carrying her cross in the procession, and all the times she came to my studio to sit to me, and the night of the Westcreek ball

—I was quite on a wrong scent then—do you remember? I don't think I ever was happier than for that year or two I spent down there. And that reminds me—I wish you would get me a pen and ink and a bit of paper. I always meant to add a codicil to my will to leave a trifle to my good old Peninah; she was a kind soul to me, and I should not like her to be forgotten. One puts things off so unless one happens to be ill. Just a memorandum to my executor will be enough; he will act upon it all right. My writing-case is over there on that table in the corner."

"My dear fellow, there is no occasion to worry yourself about that now. You will be all right in the morning, and can do it much better by daylight. I was wrong to let you get talking of things and exciting yourself. Your hand is shaking now. Lie down, and let me cover you over."

"Not till I have had my way. It won't take a minute, and then it will be off my mind."

He was so peremptory, and looked so flushed, that Studland thought it better not to thwart him; but when it was done he gave him his draught and insisted on his trying to sleep, withdrawing to the other side of the room that there might be less temptation to talk. There seemed no sleep, however, in the wide shining eyes that were always watching him whenever he looked round, and by-and-by he asked him whether there was any one he would like written to.

"I don't like leaving you to this strange nurse," he said; "and I am afraid I must go back on Monday."

"No, thanks," was the answer; "there is no one I should care to bother. The Wynnstays are in Algiers, or Hugh would come to me at a minute's notice, I know. My aunt's address is on the mantelshelf; she must be written to, of course, if 'anything should happen,' as the poor folks put it. If nothing does, I shall do very well alone. But I am awfully grateful to you for stopping with me to-night," he added.

Presently he asked if it were not nearly morning yet, and Studland, drawing aside the curtain, let in the view of the sea, turning opal in the earliest light of dawn. The sick man lay watching it till he dropped asleep with the sunshine on his face. He was sleeping still when the nurse arrived by the first train, and Alick, having given over his charge, slipped noiselessly away without farewell.

When a little later he sent up to inquire, the answer was—not quite so well. The nurse thought he had better not be disturbed, so finding he was of no use, he went off for a long stretch across the wide boggy heath that borders Poole Harbour. He intended to be back early, but thinking deeply as he walked of the strange talk he had had with Kay last night, he went further than he thought, and getting perplexed with the incoming tide, had to make a long detour, and to his vexation found he had been out some hours. When he got in, his first inquiry was for Kay. The waiter looked round before he answered, and then drew him mysteriously into the office.

"He is dead, sir. He died about an hour ago. Would you like to see the nurse?"

Was it possible? Dead! so soon; he had never thought the illness was so serious as this. It seemed impossible to realize. He stood there waiting, his unseeing eyes fixed on the framed and glazed advertisements of clarets and bourdeaux with which the walls were adorned, until the nurse appeared—a business-like looking young woman, with her starched lappets and bunch of scissors and knives dangling from her waist by steel chains.

"Yes," she said in answer to his shocked query, "he went off very sudden. He had been getting worse all day, but neither the doctor nor I thought there was any danger; but in these cases you never can tell; different people take the complaint so differently. I suppose his friends ought to have been sent for, but there was no time. You will excuse my being in rather a hurry, sir; I am anxious to get back to town to-night. It was really a pity I came; it was not worth while sending for me for such a short case. I should have thought Dr. Parker might have found some one in the place who would have done very well; but I suppose it will be a satisfaction to the relatives to know that he had every possible attention."

"I have no wish to detain you," said Studland,

curtly, "but I should like to hear a few particulars. Was he conscious at the last?"

"Naturally you would, sir, but there is really nothing to tell. He took his beef-tea about an hour before, and then asked me to raise him up upon the pillows that he might look out at the sea. He appeared to be a very silent gentleman; but it seemed to amuse him to watch the boats. I noticed when I lifted him that though he had been ill so short a time, he was as weak as a baby and wonderfully light. I took a book, hoping he might drop off to sleep, and all of a sudden he called me, and I thought he was going to faint; I gave him a spoonful of brandy as quick as I could, but it was no use; he was gone. No; he never asked for any one, nor sent a message, nor said a word to show he thought himself in any danger. Indeed, he scarcely spoke to me except to ask for what he wanted, and that was little enough; he was no trouble."

She glanced restlessly at the clock as she finished speaking, and Alick gladly took the hint and dismissed her. He felt a lump rising in his throat as he thought of poor Kay left to such hired ministrations as these, and wished with remorseful pain that he had never left him. If the woman had been more gentle and tender it would not have seemed so piteous, but evidently to her it was "a case," and hardly troublesome enough to be worth the expenditure of her trained skill. He would have liked to go into the room to see him once more, but the undertaker's women were already in possession; he must wait.

He had no time to think about the pathos of it all; he must see the doctor and the manager of the hotel, and telegraph to the relations in London. He found there was just time to send off a telegram before the post-office closed, and he was coming out after having dispatched it, when he caught sight of a lady putting a letter in the box. He looked again. Yes, his eyes had not deceived him; it was Jenifer. He made one step to her side.

"Miss Lyon, is it really you?"

She started. "Captain Studland! I had no idea you were in Bournemouth. We are staying till Monday. They all say I want more fresh air, so we thought it would be a good plan while my Saturday engagement lasts to spend the Sunday here by the sea. We are in lodgings close by. Frau Klieschmann is gone to evening service, but I was tired, and I only just slipped out to post my letters. In lodgings they always expect you to do that for yourself. How odd I should have met you."

Then something in his look, and in his silence, struck her, and she asked quickly—

"Is anything the matter?"

"Yes," he answered gravely; "something very sad has just happened; something that you will be grieved to hear. I should like to tell you about it."

"Come in with me, then. Our rooms are just here."

He followed her, but did not speak till they stood in the little drawing-room, dim with firelight. Jenifer did not light the lamp, but turned to him at once.

"What is it?" she said.

"Did you know that Kay was here ill?"

"No. Is it very serious? Is there anything I can do?"

"Nothing. There is nothing that any one can do for him any more; he died this afternoon."

"Oh, poor Denis. I hardly know how to believe it; he always seemed so young, and full of life How grievous. Tell me all about it."

They sat down side by side on the little sofa, and in a low voice he told her all there was to tell. As he spoke, she drew out her handkerchief, and as the firelight flickered on her face he could see that she was crying; but those pitiful, tender-hearted tears gave him no jealous pang; he would not have had her listen dry-eyed. His own eyes were wet, and his voice shook and grew a little husky.

"He spoke of you last night," he said. "Some day perhaps I will tell you what he said, but not now. No, it was not a message, or you should have it at once. I am glad I met you, and was able to tell you. He would not have liked you to hear it suddenly or see it in the papers."

"He was always very good to me," she said.

Alick rose. "I ought to go now; there may be things to see to."

"Must you? I suppose you must. Thanks for coming in. I am so glad you were with him last night. I cannot bear to think of him dying so unfriended. I wish I had known he was ill; it seems so horrible for me to have been fiddling away at the concert while he lay dying."

When he was gone, she came back to the fire and cried a little more; but her tears were not all for Denis. The ghost of the old dead love rose up and troubled her. Alick looked very sad and worn; she wondered whether he were grieving for Letty still.

CHAPTER IX.

THEY were walking side by side along the level sandy cliff leading from Bournemouth to Boscombe — Jenifer and Alick Studland — as they had often walked together in a very different scene. Inland the mean straggling suburbs of the elder mushroom almost joined the unfinished outskirts of the new. It would be difficult to say which of the two was most depressing in its ugliness. Even the very sea itself seemed a poor thing compared with the grand Atlantic, with its far-reaching billows, its melting shades of emerald and amethyst; here the coastline was so straight, the shallow waves which rolled in upon the sand, so tame, so blue, so monotonous. But to Alick it mattered nothing; for Jenifer was beside him, and the sea-colour was in her eyes.

It was Sunday afternoon. Only two days since they laid Denis Kay in the crowded churchyard by the sea, and Studland, who had come to attend the funeral, had got his leave extended over the Sunday—on urgent private affairs—that he might see Jenifer again. They had been talking of Denis; of his genius and of the strange way in which his thread of life had been cut just when it seemed as though he might accomplish such great things. His renown and success had been growing fast these three years, and it seemed sad that all should be so suddenly extinguished.

"But I suppose," said Jenifer, "that his work was really done; and truly he had accomplished more in his brief three and thirty years than most men do in a long life."

She felt his death deeply, for though she had not been able to give him that which he craved, her friendship and regard had been his in full measure.

"The other night," she was saying, as they came down the formal paths of what once was Boscombe Chine, "you told me that he spoke of me. Won't you tell me what he said? Was it anything he wanted me to do for him?"

"I am not quite ready to tell you yet. I want to ask you something first."

He looked round discontentedly upon the crowds of 'Arries with their sweethearts, who on a Sunday afternoon poured out in endless succession from the Bournemouth shops.

"What a rabble! Can't we get away from it all? The end of the pier seems tolerably deserted. Would it be too cold for you there?"

"Not at all, thanks; I should like it."

She wondered as they walked down the monotonous length what he could possibly have to say to her, and why he did not begin. No suspicion of what it was ever dawned upon her. Her utter unconsciousness made it much harder for him. He could not help recollecting how fatally easy it had been to slide into a declaration once, when he had but half meant it; and now, when he wanted to express the craving of his whole nature, he was dumb. At last, when they reached the end, and paused leaning over the balustrade to watch the dull ripples swirling among the piles, he found speech.

"Jenifer," he began—he had not for a long time called her by her name—"I feel at such a disadvantage, I hardly know how to begin. Perhaps I am wrong to speak so soon; I have not had a chance to make you understand what is in my heart, but it is no use waiting; you won't give me the chance; you hold me off so. I don't believe it is any use; yet I must tell you, I love you. Is there any hope for me?"

For a minute Jenifer stood as if turned to stone. Was this true, or was she dreaming? They say all things come round to those who wait; but some things come too late.

It seemed a long while, it was really only a moment or two before she drew a long breath, and said—

"I am very sorry. No, it cannot be."

"Won't you give me any reason?"

"It is simply that I don't mean to marry. I have chosen my part; I have my work; I mean to live for that."

He brushed this reason aside, as if it had been a cobweb.

"Ah, if that were all," he said. "But I ought not to wonder at your feeling that the love cannot be worth having that was offered so lately to another woman. It was foolish of me to be so precipitate; I ought to have waited to convince you of the reality of what I feel for you. You still think of me as Letty's lover."

"It is not that kind of feeling at all," said Jenifer, with a sort of perplexity; "though truly I think you may be mistaken."

"Mistaken! I dare say. A man who is starving may be mistaken in fancying that it is bread he wants. Still, I know I have laid myself open to the reproach of not knowing my own mind. Will you let me try and tell you a little about myself? You have known so much about me, perhaps if I could make you understand it all I might have a better chance."

She acquiesced, and he went on—

"I dare say you never guessed that years ago, when you were almost a little girl, I was in love with you." He was watching the effect of his words, and he could have fancied he saw a light like dawn cross her face for an instant. "I was not in a position to marry; it seemed to me wrong that I should try to bind you. I never said anything, but I waited and hoped; and I did fancy you cared for me a little then. You remember the time? It was when I came home from the

West Indies. But when I came back at Christmas, I found you absorbed as it seemed to me with poor Kay and his picture, and I was told you were on the brink of becoming engaged to him. I saw you wearing his pearls, and that was confirmation to my mind. I had no right to reproach you; I had no manner of claim. If there had ever been anything between us I might have asked you to explain; as it was, I simply tried to put you out of my mind. Later, when I was home invalided, the same bugbear stood between us, and—well, I need not go into the folly of that summer. I am not going to pretend to you that I never cared for Mrs. Dendron; but there are more ways than one of caring, and it was not the sort of thing that lasts. We ought never to have been engaged; it came about, I can hardly tell you how; I scarcely knew myself. I only know what a reprieve it was when she threw me over; for in the meanwhile I had seen you again."

He waited a little, but Jenifer did not speak, and he went on—

"Jenifer, can't you forgive me? Can you never forgive me?"

"Oh, you don't understand. It is not a question of forgiving; how could it be? It is simply that I have grown happy and content with the life that I have chosen. I will not be disturbed with this. Please let me be."

He was perplexed. "Will you tell me one thing?" he asked. "Does the memory of Denis

Kay—does the thought of any other man stand between you and me?"

"Neither Denis nor any man," she answered. "Do you think a woman can never be sufficient to herself?"

He passed the question by.

"You asked me just now to tell you what it was he said to me about you the night before he died; it was to bid me hope."

"You told him?"

"No, not exactly; he divined it. Whether it was our being thrown together by such an odd chance, or whether death drawing near made him strangely clear sighted, I don't understand; but he roused up to talk of you. He told me he had failed, and he called me a fool for thinking I had no chance. But for that I should hardly have had the courage to speak now. Was he mistaken? Was I mistaken in fancying that I might have made you care for me once? Are you angry with me, Jenifer, for telling you?"

"No, not angry. You have been very candid with me, Alick, and I do not see why I should not be so too. It is true I loved you once years ago, though I did not think anybody could have guessed it. I was almost a child then, and knew so little how much things meant. I was very silly; I thought you liked me, and when you changed it was very terrible to me. You see it is such a shame to a woman to have been mistaken on such a point. My one idea was that you should never know—no one should ever know. I had nearly betrayed myself that night of the shipwreck, when you went out with the lifeboat, and I could not stay quietly in the cottage waiting with the others; but luckily for me you went away very soon after, and I had a little time. When you came again, my pride had grown stronger, and when I saw you fascinated with Mrs. Dendron, what could I do but strangle whatever feeling was left alive? It took a long while dying, but it is dead now."

She had spoken without looking towards him; her eyes were fixed on the sharp serrated outline of the Needles, standing white against the leaden autumnal sky. She kept them steadily there.

He laid his hand on hers.

"Since you loved me once, Jenifer, I shall never give up hope, however long I may have to wait."

"It is no use. It has become a fixed habit with me to try always to keep out of your way; never to talk of you, never to think of you if I could possibly help it. What sort of wife should I make? No, leave me to my music."

"And does that wholly content you?"

"If it does not, it makes me forget that I am not contented. It occupies me and satisfies me. And what do I want more?"

"I want a good deal more; and I mean to have it. No, Jenifer, I do not fear such a shadowy rival as your violin. You may refuse me this time, and send me away; but I shall have you for my wife yet."

She met his eyes, and her own fell. The resolute tone of his voice almost frightened her. She rose hastily.

"Come, let us go home. I am cold."

"I am so sorry; I ought not to have let you sit so long in this bitter wind, but I could not remember anything while all my thoughts were set to winning you. I had no notion it was so late."

The early November twilight was creeping in over the sea, and low in the west, behind the pinewoods, the sun had left long crimson streaks between the grey. 'Arry and his young woman had gone in to tea, and the path by the cliffs was desolate. They walked on together very silently, for ordinary talk was hardly possible just now. At last, however, he broke the silence.

"How still it is after the rabble of this afternoon. Couldn't you almost fancy yourself at Kerranstow, on the Parson's Walk above the Shag's Head?"

"I miss the sound, though. Don't you know how on the calmest day the sea comes with such a boom into the caves. Often at Wimmelhahn the silence used to wake me in the middle of the night, as noise might any one else. I hardly feel as if I was by the sea with that mild little swish swish."

"Some day," he said, "you and I will stand together on your little platform where the brook goes down, and listen to the old sound once more.

Ah, Jenifer, how much we have wasted and lost of what we might have enjoyed together. Don't let us throw away any more of it by needless hesitations."

She made no answer to that; she felt he was getting an advantage by taking things for granted so; and she felt that he was stronger than she. They walked on in silence for a little distance. Presently he spoke again.

"I am not much by way of quoting books; but the other night, when I was sitting up with Kay, I took up a story that was lying there, and dipped into it. There was one sentence that stuck by me, and I should like to tell it to you. It was this— 'New love is brightest, and long love is greatest; but revived love is the tenderest thing known upon the earth.'"

CHAPTER X.

IT was only a question of time; Jenifer herself must have known it, though she held out long and stubbornly. She hardly knew whether she most dreaded loving Alick, or not loving him; whether she most feared to let the old feeling revive, and so put herself at his mercy again, or distrusted her power of restoring the affection she had strangled. One thing was very certain; the time for putting him out of her thoughts was quite gone by. She might try to forget their talk on the pier at Boscombe, but it would not be ignored, and came back to her again and again. Moreover, his avowal that he had loved her in those early days, to which she had learned to look back with so much shame, had healed her of the shrinking with which she had always turned away from the recollection; the love she had battled with had, after all, not been founded on a delusion; she could think of him without any humiliation now.

If she had seen more of him she would probably have yielded sooner; but their meetings were brief and unsatisfactory. He was a good deal tied just now to his ship, and it frequently happened that just when he had fixed to run up to town for the day, orders would come sending the *Wildcat*, the gun-boat of which he was in command, off to Portland, or for a cruise to Ireland, and then when he could get away, he would find Jenifer in a whirl of engagements.

For she was getting very busy as the winter went on. She made her *début* at St. James's Hall under most favourable auspices; gave a recital at the Langham; and was getting every week more and more engagements to play at At Homes; in short, she was becoming the fashion, and "Have you heard Miss Lyon?" was getting to be quite one of the stock questions. She and Frau Klieschmann had taken a charming little flat in Kensington, and were making many friends in that pleasant borderland which is not quite the fashionable, nor quite the artistic world, but partakes a little of both. Alick grew discouraged sometimes.

One evening she was dressing for a concert, to which she was going in the capacity of listener instead of performer. Nicolai, who had devoted his winter to Berlin, had just come to town for the season, and was playing in St. James's Hall. Jenifer never missed an opportunity of hearing her master; it was a fresh inspiration to her every time she listened to him.

"You are getting quite thin, Miss Jenifer," said the maid, who was lacing her dress. "I am sure you work too hard. You ought to give yourself a little rest. I really shall have to take in this gown before you wear it again."

"Oh, I shall soon fatten up in the summer, when I go home to Roscorla and eat Cornish cream. London gives one no time to get fat. There is some one at the door, Penfold. Just see if it is letters, and I can read them while you finish me."

The maid went to see, and came back with an exquisite nosegay of white lilac, loosely tied together with pale green ribbons, a note, and two letters by the post.

"Ah, I know who that is from!" said Jenifer, taking the flowers, and burying her nose in the fresh sweetness. "How German, and how kind of Herr Nicolai. That is to remind me to come, I suppose."

She opened his note first.

"In case I don't see you to-night," she read, "I write to ask if I may bring Gregorio to call on you on Friday. I know it is not your At Home day; but he is a busy man, and I think he may put something good in your way."

Gregorio was a noted impresario; that he should wish to call upon her was an honour she was fully alive to. She owed it to Nicolai, she knew. Then she went on to open the other two. The next bore a St. Petersburg postmark. Letty had kept up a correspondence, and was always urging Jenifer to try her luck in the Russian capital. The letter was full of enthusiastic descriptions of the winter life there, which seemed to suit the writer exactly. Near the end she said—

"Certainly happiness does not come only to those that deserve it; for I have deserved anything rather, and I am more happy than I can say. And yet I think it makes me feel more penitent than if I had been punished. Do you ever hear anything of poor Alick? Was he very miserable? Do you think he is getting over it?"

"Poor Alick, indeed!" Jenifer indignantly tossed the letter away and opened his, which she had kept till the last.

"I have been horribly disappointed about coming up to town this week. I have just got a fortnight's leave, but my poor old stepfather is very failing, and Rachel wants me. I suppose there is no chance of your taking a holiday, and coming down to Roscorla? If you only would. You looked as if you wanted rest badly last time I saw you."

The sound of a bell disturbed her. They were expecting friends to dine and go with them to the concert. She thrust the letters into her pocket, took up her fragrant bouquet, and went into the other room.

Nicolai was at his best that night; he always was when he numbered his favourite pupil among his hearers. Fine performer as he invariably showed himself, he needed something more than admiration—he wanted at least one sympathetic listener to draw out the second self that lay hid in the virtuoso, and gave him at times such a magical power. When his audience was cold, he treated them to a marvellous display of gymnastics, as brilliant and chilly as frost; it needed the other pole of the magnetic current to set free all the passion and sweetness of which he was capable. This it was which gave people such contradictory opinions of him—"Magnificent, but soulless," some would say, and others—"He carries one fairly off one's feet with excitement." His restless black eyes would rove over the sea of faces, till they lighted on one who was listening with his soul as well as with his bodily ears, and to that one he played. But when Jenifer was there he was content. "Sit where I can see you," he sometimes said to her. "I like to know that some one is really listening among all these deaf adders who come because it is the thing to hear me—and then encore the singer."

Jenifer herself felt quite differently. While she played, the crowded hall became to her simply a large coloured mass in which she never attempted to discriminate, and she withdrew into a world where she and the composer had it to themselves. Had it not been for her power to do this, she would hardly have had the nerve to face a London audience. But she understood her master's need, and ministered to it whenever she could.

He had chosen many of her best loved things, and as he played the conviction grew on her stronger and stronger that, after all, music was the only thing worth living for. While one listened to such strains as these, one was in heaven, and the outside world was but a vain show. But presently, for an encore, he played a nocturne of his own; one which he had written for her, dedicated to her, and which she had played at Exeter that night when Alick and Mr. Jaques had gone to hear her. The spell of association was strong; the thought of Alick came up and strove with the other. There was a tender longing about the refrain which thrilled her. The music rose to a rhapsody of yearning and struggle and pain, and then sank down again to the stillness of the opening passage. It seemed as though through it she could hear Alick saying to her—"But revived love is the tenderest thing known upon the earth."

And so, all unwitting, Nicolai gave his best pupil away.

Coming out, he overtook them in the corridor.

"You had my note?" he said.

"Yes, thanks so much, and for these exquisite flowers too. I have not had time to answer it yet. I am so sorry; I should have been so pleased; but I shall not be in town on Friday; I am going home to-morrow for ten days."

"Must you go? Can't you put it off a day or two? You may miss a good chance, if you miss Gregorio."

"I am afraid I can't. I want a little rest very badly, and I have just this little interval without engagements, at least without any I cannot put off, and it won't happen again before the rush of the season."

He looked vexed. As he put her in the cab she leaned forward.

"Please don't think me ungrateful. I do thank you so very much for all your goodness to me."

He stood a moment on the pavement looking after the cab, puzzled.

"What can she have meant by taking such a solemn farewell? Women are queer, unaccountable creatures. I suppose she has got something on her nerves, and had better go into the country if she has set her heart upon it; but it is a pity."

"My dear," said Frau Klieschmann, as they drove off, "you took me quite by surprise. Was I not discreet not to say a word? but I had not an idea you were thinking of going into the country before the summer."

"I am so sorry," said Jenifer, penitently; "it was very wrong of me; but I only decided it this evening, partly because of some letters I got while I was dressing, and then the Smith Bagots dining with us made it impossible for me to say anything. I should not have told Herr Nicolai but for his wanting to bring Gregorio on Friday. Shall you mind my leaving you alone? It will only be for ten days."

But when Jenifer found herself at home once more, and, fencing with the surprised queries of her relations, realized what had brought her, she had almost made up her mind to go back to town the next day. If it had been a shorter journey, she probably would have fled; but one does not travel down to the West for nothing, and being there, she needs must abide what the fates would bring.

One thing she could not do, and that was to sit quietly in the green rep drawing-room, and await a possible call from Captain Studland under the beady eyes of Louisa. She suggested a drive into Widcombe, but the cob was wanted on the farm, and Louisa said, with not unnatural astonishment—

"My dear, what can you possibly want to buy in those poky little shops, when you have but just come from London?"

Mrs. Lyon proposed that if she wanted a walk she should go up to Hennacombe to see Miss Treby, and inquire for the old gentleman. He had had a slight stroke, but was getting about again; still they ought to inquire; they had not heard how he was the last day or two. This was the most impossible suggestion of all, and with a hasty and incoherent excuse about wanting to see Mr. Jaques, she set off in the direction of Kerranstow.

It was Friday, however, and Friday was his sermon day, as she presently recollected; she must not disturb him yet. Neither would she go down to any of her old haunts on the cliffs. Alick knew them all, and would be sure to seek her there, and she had a perfectly unreasonable feeling that to let him find her would be granting too much. She turned into the churchyard, and seated herself on the stile formed of a slab of granite set edgewise, which separated God's acre from the cliff. On the slope above her, against the background of dark yews, stood the huge and shapeless figure of Freia, rudely carved in wood, and once painted and gilded, though now bleached and weather stained with many a winter's exposure—strange monument for a Christian graveyard, yet how appropriate—watching over the last sleep of Captain Eric Magnus and his eleven Norse sailors, lying side by side below.

It was very still; from the wind-blown elms that sheltered one side of the church the rooks were beginning to caw, and getting busy over their nest-building, and overhead a long troop of little fleecy white clouds, like a flock of sheep, seemed pasturing in the wide field of blue. As she watched them dreamily, she was going over to herself the scene that she knew was before her. She was well aware how it must end now: by coming down she cut off her own retreat. She almost wished she had not been so hasty to yield to his entreaty; she wondered how she should meet him, and what she should say. She tried to recall what she had said to him that autumn Sunday afternoon; but the thing she could not recall was the numb state of feeling that had given her firmness then.

Still as it was, she did not hear the sound of footsteps over the short turf behind her, and almost before she knew any one was there, Alick was holding her fast, and his voice was in her ear.

"So you have come to me at last. I knew you would not be here if you did not mean that."

The time had gone by for hesitations or doubts. She looked up at him.

"I could not help coming, Alick. I told you once my love was dead, but I found it was not true."

* * * * * *

The vicar was walking up and down the terrace with Samuel at his heels as of old. The sermon had been thought out, and he was musing of many things. John was cutting the grass on the slope above. Passers-by were not so frequent that they could be unobserved, and when two black figures cut the sky-line, going down over the shoulder of Corbie Crag, both master and man paused to look after them. One was Alick Studland, by the russet shooting-coat, but who was the other? Not Rachel, and, moreover, there was something in the walk of these two, in the way the head of the taller bent towards the other, that suggested lovers.

"John," said the vicar, "did you notice who that was that went over the hill with Captain Studland, just now?"

And John, whose eyes were as long-sighted as those of a Red Indian, answered without hesitation, "Why, that was Miss Jenifer, sir."

"Ah."

There was a world of surprise and satisfaction in the monosyllable.

John leaned upon his scythe, his eyes still following the vanishing figures.

"God bless them! 'Tis what always ought to ha' been from the beginning; but 'tis a queer world. If the right thing ever does happen, seemin'ly 'tis bound to go wrong first."

And with this piece of philosophy John returned to his mowing.

* * * * * *

"Ah," said Nicolai, throwing down a letter in which Jenifer announced to him her changed prospects; "so that was why she would not see Gregorio. What a chance she threw away!"

He flicked the ash off the end of his cigar meditatively.

"I am a fool to be disappointed. She was only a woman, after all."

THE END.

PRINTED BY WILLIAM CLOWES AND SONS, LIMITED.
LONDON AND BECCLES. *G., C. & Co.*

www.ingramcontent.com/pod-product-compliance
Lightning Source LLC
Chambersburg PA
CBHW020756230426
43666CB00007B/724